AF673650

FEMINISM AND ANTHROPOLOGICAL THEORY

FEMINISM AND ANTHROPOLOGICAL THEORY

Shoumitra Verma

MD PUBLICATIONS PVT LTD
NEW DELHI
www.mdppl.com

Copyright © 2010 by MD Publications Pvt Ltd.

All rights reserved. No part of this book may be reproduced or utilized in any form or by any means, electronically or mechanically, including photocopying, recording, or by any information storage and retrieval system, without the prior permission in writing from the publisher.

Published by:

MD Publications Pvt Ltd
"MD House", 11, Darya Ganj,
New Delhi - 110 002
Phone : +91-11-45355555
E-mail : contact@mdppl.com
website : www.mdppl.com

ISBN: 978-81-7533-296-6

Published and Printed by Mr. Pranav Gupta on behalf of **MD Publications Pvt Ltd** at JJ offset Printers, Delhi.

Preface

The subfield of Feminist Anthropology emerged in the early 1970s as a reaction to a perceived androcentric bias within the discipline. Two related points should be made concerning this reaction. First of all, some of the prominent figures in early American anthropology (i.e. Margaret Mead and Ruth Benedict) were women, and the discipline has traditionally been more egalitarian, in terms of gender, than other social sciences. Underlying that statement, however, is the fact that the discipline has been subject to prevailing modes of thought through time and has certainly exhibited the androcentric thinking which early feminist anthropologists accused it of.

The first feminist anthropologists perceived substantial gaps in the corpus of anthropological literature as a result of male bias. What ethnographic data concerning women that existed was often, in reality, the reports of male informants transmitted through male ethnographers.

Feminist anthropology has contributed a diverse group of voices to the field from the point of view of the researcher, in addition to representing voices from a plethora of different groups of women. As part of a broader feminist project, it has been a part of the promotion of women voices and interests, insisting that women be heard, even when they may have to take more subtle approaches to authority through acts of resistance.

Contemporary feminist anthropologists are no longer focusing their research solely on the issue of gender asymmetry. Instead they have begun to explore the importance of female activities, such as "foraging, parenting, and sexual selection in our reconstructions of human history". The focus has shifted towards more particularistic and historically grounded studies that place gender at the center of analysis. Issues significant to women of color, lesbians, and Third World peoples are now recognized and incorporated into the scholarship produced by feminist anthropologists.

Feminist anthropology has been criticized for a number of issues since its emergence in the 1970s. One early criticism was made by female anthropologists belonging to ethnic minorities. Their criticism was that white, middle class female anthropologists were focusing too intensely on issues of gender. Consequently, the subfield was ignoring social inequalities arising from issues such as racism and the unequal distribution of wealth. This criticism has been redressed both by a heightened awareness of such issues by the aforementioned white, middle class feminist anthropologists, as well as the entry of large numbers of minority anthropologists into the field.

I am very grateful to Mr. Pranav Gupta, Director of MD Publications Pvt Ltd, New Delhi, for his kind cooperation and support for this book.

Shoumitra Verma

CONTENTS

1

Feminist Anthropology
Basic Premises

The subfield of Feminist Anthropology emerged in the early 1970s as a reaction to a perceived androcentric bias within the discipline (Lamphere 1996: 488). Two related points should be made concerning this reaction. First of all, some of the prominent figures in early American anthropology (i.e. Margaret Mead and Ruth Benedict) were women, and the discipline has traditionally been more egalitarian, in terms of gender, than other social sciences (di Leonardo 1991: 5-6). Underlying that statement, however, is the fact that the discipline has been subject to prevailing modes of thought through time and has certainly exhibited the androcentric thinking which early feminist anthropologists accused it of (Reiter 1975: 13-14).

The first feminist anthropologists perceived substantial gaps in the corpus of anthropological literature as a result of male bias (Lamphere 1996: 488). What ethnographic data concerning women that existed was often, in reality, the reports of male informants transmitted through male ethnographers (Pine 1996: 253). Contemporary feminist anthropologists are no longer focusing their research solely on the issue of gender asymmetry. Instead they have begun to explore the importance of female activities, such as "foraging, parenting, and sexual selection in our reconstructions of human history"(McGee and Warms 1996:391). The focus has shifted towards more particularistic and historically grounded studies that place gender at the center of analysis. Issues significant to women of color, lesbians, and Third World peoples are now recognized and incorporated into the scholarship produced by feminist anthropologists (Lamphere 1996:488). This collection of work has tended to follow a few main trends. The first trend developed along a materialistic perspective. Several of the scholars who follow this perspective focus on gender as it relates to class, the social relations of power, and changes in modes of production. The second of these trends focuses on "the social construction of gender as it is expressed in the roles of motherhood, kinship, and marriage" (McGee and Warms 1996:392).

In general, contemporary feminist anthropologists have shown that gender is an important analytical concept (McGee and Warms 1996:392). Gender is a term that came into popular use in the early 1980's. It was often found in the writings of social and cultural anthropologists. Gender was used to refer to both the male and the female, the cultural construction of these categories, and the relationship between them (Pine 1996:253). The definition of gender may vary from culture to culture, and this realization has led feminist anthropologists away from broad generalizations (Lamphere 1996:488). The focus of contemporary scholars in this area is on the differences existing among women rather than between males and females (McGee, Warms 1996: 392).

POINTS OF REACTION

Anthropology is one of the few disciplines in which women historically have been able to obtain both high levels of professional achievement and public recognition. In the anthropological literature, however, the discussion of women, until recently, has been restricted to the areas of marriage, kinship, and family. Feminist anthropologists believe that the failure of past researchers to treat the issues of women and gender as significant has led to a deficient understanding of the human experience (McGee and Warms 1996:391, from Morgen 1989:1).

One criticism made by feminist anthropologists is directed towards the language being used within the discipline. The ambiguous use of the word "man" is ambiguous, sometimes referring to *Homo sapiens* as a whole, sometimes in reference to males only, and sometimes in reference to both simultaneously. Those making this criticism cited the Sapir-Whorf hypothesis, which stated that language shapes worldview. Theorists such as S. Washburn and C. Lancaster were also criticized. In addition to using phrases such as 'poor dependent females', these theorists placed a great deal of weight on aggression. Working in the 1960's, K. Lorenz published *On Aggression* and R. Ardrey published *African Genesis*. Both were popular texts that promoted the importance of aggression in the evolutionary formation of humanity (McGee and Warms 1996:395).

A further point of reaction happened after the initial creation of the subfield. African-American anthropologists and members of other ethnic minorities were quick to point out deficiencies in the questions being asked by the early feminist anthropologists. One of those to do so was Audrey Lorde, who in a letter to Mary Daly wrote: "I feel you do celebrate differences between white women as a creative force towards change, rather than a reason for misunderstanding and separation. But you fail to recognize that, as women, those differences expose all women to various forms and degrees of patriarchal oppression, some of which we share, some of which we do not....The oppression of women knows no ethnic nor racial boundaries, true, but that does not mean it is identical within those boundaries" (Minh-ha 1989:101). Early feminist anthropologists did indeed imply, in their search for universal explanations for female subordination and gender inequality, that all women suffer the same oppression simply because we are women. The later work done in this subfield has addressed this criticism.

LEADING FIGURES

Margaret Mead's (1901-1978) theories were influenced by ideas borrowed from Gestalt psychology, that subfield of psychology which analyzed personality as an interrelated psychological pattern rather than a collection of separate elements (McGee, Warms 1996:202) Her work influenced Rosaldo's and Lamphere's attempts to build a framework for the emerging discipline. Mead's work contained an analysis of pervasive sexual asymmetry that fit with their reading of the ethnographic literature (Levinson, Ember 1996:488).

Sherry Ortner (1941-), one of the early proponents of feminist anthropology, constructed a explanatory model for gender asymmetry based on the premise that the subordination of women is a universal, that is, cross-cultural phenomenon. In an article published in 1974, Is Female to Male as Nature is to Culture?, she takes a structuralist approach to the question of gender inequality. She suggests that a woman's role as childbearer makes them natural creators, while men use are cultural creators (Ortner 1974: 77-78)).

Michelle Rosaldo, together with Ortner, offered an integrated set of explanations, each at a different level, for the universal subordination of women. These were in terms of social structure, culture, and socialization. She argued that in every society women bear and raise children and that women's socially and culturally defined role as mother provided the basis for subordination. Early feminist anthropologists such as Rosaldo did not question the concept of the universal subordination of women and used dichotomies to explain it (Lamphere 1996:488-9).

Ruth Benedict (1887-1948): Benedict, a student of Franz Boas, was an early and influential female anthropologist, earning her doctorate from Columbia University in 1923 (Buckner 1997: 34). Her fieldwork with Native Americans and other groups led her to develop the "configurational approach" to culture, seeing cultural systems as working to favor certain personality types among different societies (Buckner 1997: 34). Along with Margaret Mead she is one of the most prominent female anthropologists of the first half of this century.

KEY WORKS

Margaret Mead (1935) *Sex and Temperment in Three Primitive Societies*. New York: William Morrow. In this text Mead explores the relationship between culture and human nature. Culture is dealt with as a primary factor in determining masculine and feminine social characteristics and behavior. One of the purposes of this text was to inform Americans as to the nature of human cultural diversity (McGee and Warms 1996:202-3).

Margaret Mead (1949) *Male and Female:* A study of the sexes in a changing world. New York: Morrow Quill Paperbacks. By her own declaration, Mead attempts to do three things in this text. First, to bring a greater awareness of the way in which the differences and similarities in the bodies of human beings are the basis on which all our learning about our sex, and our relationship to the other sex, are built. Secondly, she draws on some of the knowledge we have of all human societies, to see what has been attempted in what situations, and what the results were. This is done in the hope that we might learn or be exposed to an idea that will leave us the better for it. Finally, she tries to suggest ways in which our civilization may make full use of both a man's and a woman's special talents (Mead 1949:5-6). Her analyses concerning the differences between males and females influenced many of the discussions that were to follow.

Engels, Frederick (1973) The Origin of the Family, Private Property and the State. Moscow: Progress Publishers. The theories developed by both Engels and Marx influenced many of the first feminist anthropologists. The quest for a universal understanding of female subordination, as well as the reliance upon dichotomies both had their roots in the ideas of these two men, and in the theories posited in this text.

Rosaldo, Michelle and Louise Lamphere, eds. (1974) Women, Culture, and Society. Stanford: Stanford University Press. This collection of essays emerged from a course at Stanford University, as well as from papers delivered at the

1971 American Anthropological Association meetings. These essays deal with the issue of universal sexual asymmetry, or female subordination.

Reiter, Rayna, ed. (1975) Toward an Anthropology of Women. New York: Monthly Review Press. This anthology is considered one of the groundbreaking collections of feminist essays published in the 1970's, and includes works by authors such as Sally Slocum. The ideas expressed in this collection are heavily focused towards the development of universal explanations and helpful dichotomies.

PRINCIPAL CONCEPTS

Initially, feminist anthropology focused on analysis and development of theory to explain the subordination of women, which seemed to be universal and cross-cultural. Marxist theory was appealing to feminist anthropologists in the 1970s because "there is no theory which accounts for the oppression of women – in its endless variety and monotonous similarity, cross-culturally and throughout history – with anything like the explanatory power of the Marxist theory of class oppression" (Rubin 1975: 160). The Marxist model explains that the subordination of women in capitalist societies, both in terms of their reproductive role, "the reproduction of labor," as well as their value as unpaid or underpaid labor, arises from historical trends predating capitalism itself (Rubin 1975: 160-164).

Engels, in *The Origin of the Family, Private Property, and the State*, attempted to explain the origin of these historical trends, though his 19th century theories seem dated to present day readers (Rubin 1975: 164-5). He attributed the oppression of women to shifts in the modes of production at the time of the Neolithic revolution (Rubin 1975: 169). According to Engels, once men had property (land or herds), they desired to transmit them to their offspring via patrilineal inheritance. This was accomplished by the overthrow of matrilineal inheritance and descent systems, leading to the "world historical defeat of the female sex" (Engels 1972: 120-121).

Accepting the idea that women were universally subordinated to men in some manner, anthropologists in the feminist subfield developed different models to explain this situation. Anthropologists such as Rosaldo, Edholm, and Ortner used dichotomies such as public/domestic, production/reproduction, and nature/culture (respectively) to explain universal female subordination. Ortner's use of the dichotomy to explain the universal subordination of women is built upon Levi-Strauss's conclusion that there is a universal binary opposition between nature and culture. He also argued that cross-culturally women were represented as closer to nature because of their role in reproduction (Pine 1996:254).

E. Friedl and L. Lamphere believe that, although females are subjected to universal subordination, they are not without individual power. These two anthropologists emphasize the domestic power of women. This power, according to this theoretical framework, is "manifested in individually negotiated relations based in the domestic sphere but influencing and even determining male activity in the public sphere" (Pine 1996:254).

In the late 1970's many feminist anthropologists were beginning to question the concept of universal female subordination and the usefulness of models based on dichotomies. Some anthropologists argued that there existed societies where males and females held roles that were complementary but equal. The work done by A. Schlegal and J. Briggs in foraging and tribal societies is an example of this. K. Sacks used a modes-of-production analysis to show that "hunter-gatherers possessed a communal political economy in which sisters, wives, brothers, and husbands all had the same relation to productive means and resources". Another criticism made against the use of dichotomies was that these dichotomies were Western categories. They, therefore, are not applicable to cross-cultural studies and analyses (Lamphere 1996:489).

The use and development of the concept 'gender ' has helped to further separate feminist anthropology from the use of dichotomies and the search for universals. Gender, as it came to replace the term woman in the anthropological discussions, helped to free the issue of inequality from biological connotations. These new discussions of gender brought with them more complex issues of cross-cultural translation, universality, the relationship between thought systems and individual action, and between ideology and material conditions (Pine 1996: 255). I. Illich defines sex as the "duality that stretches toward the illusory goal of economic, political, legal, or social equality between women and men". He defines gender as the "eminently local and time bound duality that sets off men and women under circumstances and conditions that prevent them from saying, doing, desiring, or perceiving 'the same thing'" (Minh-ha 1989:105).

METHODOLOGIES

The unifying aspect of feminist anthropology is that it focuses on the role, status, and contributions of women to their societies. Within this framework, individual anthropologists explore a wide range of interests and employ a wide range of theoretical models to interpret data. It would, consequently, be problematic to characterize any one approach or model as predominant within the field at present.

That observation aside, however, one should note that the field was more unified during its early development in the 1970s, when the interest was on developing models to explain the universal subordination of women. The preferred theoretical framework to analyze this state of affairs was Marxist. This preference stemmed both from the utility of the Marxist model for the analysis of gender asymmetry, as well as the early foundational writings of Marx and Engels concerning the status of women in capitalist economic systems.

Within the Marxist framework, the oppression of women is carried out by men in support of the capitalist system (Rubin 1975: 164-5). They maintain that the oppression of women supports capitalism on two levels: first of all, women serve as the mean of reproducing the labor force. Additionally, however, women's unpaid or underpaid labor serves to help defray and conceal the overall cost of operating a capitalist economy, thereby elevating profit margins for the bourgeoisie (Rubin 1975: 164-5).

Initial explanatory models to account for female oppression also took a structuralist approach. Within these models, the roles of men and women were seen as being culturally constructed. The reproductive functions of women and men historically led to the association of women with lower-status, but relatively safer, activities within the domestic sphere, the village, or other setting. At the same time, men's role in reproduction allowed them (or forced them) to operate outside of "safe" spatial areas. These dichotomous orientations managed to outlive the environmental pressures which originally prompted their adoption.

Both the Marxist model and the structuralist model reject the notion that the oppression of women is associated with something innate and biological about the human species. Sexual dimorphism in humans is a biological feature of the species but serves only to facilitate the possible oppression of women, not to mandate it or program such behavior into humans (Leibowitz 1975: 20-1). Mead's ethnographic research examined cultures where male and female behavior was inconsistent with the western conception of rational males and emotional females, for instance (Leibowitz 1975: 20-1). Likewise, primate studies demonstrate widely varying forms of interaction between male and female apes (Leibowitz 1975: 25-31).

ACCOMPLISHMENTS

The most obvious contribution of feminist anthropology has been the increased awareness of women within anthropology, both in terms of ethnographic accounts and theory. This emphasis has challenged a number of enshrined beliefs, for instance concerning models of human origins wherein the "man the hunter" model was seen as being the driving force in human evolution, ignoring the role that women's productive and reproductive roles in the evolution of Homo sapiens sapiens (Conkey and Williams 1991: 116-7). Feminist anthropology has been intimately tied to the study of gender and its construction by various societies, an interest that examines both women and men (di Leonardo 1991: 1).

CRITICISMS

Feminist anthropology has been criticized for a number of issues since its emergence in the 1970s. One early criticism, noted above, was made by female anthropologists belonging to ethnic minorities. Their criticism was that white, middle class female anthropologists were focusing too intensely on issues of gender. Consequently, the subfield was ignoring social inequalities arising from issues such as racism and the unequal distribution of wealth. This criticism has been redressed both by a heightened awareness of such issues by the aforementioned white, middle class feminist anthropologists, as well as the entry of large numbers of minority anthropologists into the field.

Additionally, feminist anthropology has been accused of mirroring the situation they originally criticized. The field began as a critique of the androcentric bias deriving from men (male ethnographers) studying men (male informants). However, it has often been the case that feminist anthropology consists of women studying women in the same arrangement. The field has attempted to address this issue by focusing more broadly on the issue of gender and moving away from the "Anthropology of Women" (di Leonardo 1991: 1).

Finally, the field has always been intimately associated with the Feminist Movement and has often been politicized. This practice is problematic on a number of levels. For one, it alienates many from the field by projecting an aura of radicalism. For another, putting politics before attempts at impartial inquiry tends to lead to research of questionable merit.

THREE GENERATIONS OF WOMEN ANTHROPOLOGISTS

The professional lives of Alice Fletcher, Harriet Cosgrove, and Cora Du Bois span more than one hundred years of

American Anthropology. All three were closely associated with the Peabody Museum which, along with the Tozzer Library, holds many of the letters, notebooks, photographs, artifacts, and publications that allow us to trace their individual histories as well as the history of the discipline they helped to shape.

The careers of these women reflect the times they lived, however, the professional and personal choices they made were uniquely their own. Fletcher, Cosgrove, and Du Bois were not, strictly speaking, institutional scholars. Due to prejudice, personal leanings, and the predilections of powerful mentors, they worked for all or most of their careers without the security of tenure or regular university appointments.

Each of these women possessed a special talent for inventing themselves as they crafted their individual relationships to the discipline of Anthropology. The roads they took were unusual-perhaps even eccentric-but in making their own way they established methods of working that have enriched those who followed them. Whether our attention is drawn to Fletcher's transcription of Omaha music, Cosgrove's painstaking documentation of Mimbres pottery, or Du Bois's pioneering use of photography, we must be impressed by the uniqueness of their visions and the strength of their commitment to anthropology.

Alice Fletcher

Alice Fletcher (1838-1923) started her anthropological career at the age of 40 so that, she reports, she could make something of herself. By 1880, Fletcher had become a regular visitor at the Peabody Museum and was assigned a place at Lucien Carr's worktable where she learned the careful research methods that were the hallmark of Frederick Putnam's apprenticeships.

Fletcher began her research in the Great Plains in 1881. During the next four decades she observed, analyzed, and published accounts of the rituals, music, dance, and social life of the Omaha, Sioux, Pawnee, and Nez Perce. She collected artifacts for the Peabody Museum, where she held an endowed fellowship from 1890-1923, and worked as a government agent allotting reservation land to individual Indians. Fletcher held strong assimilationist views and was convinced that survival for the Indians meant individual survival-not the persistence of tribal groups which she was convinced were dead or dying.

Fletcher authored-and co-authored with Francis La Flesche, her informally adopted son and one of the first Native American Anthropologists in the United States-some of the most enduring accounts of Plains cultures. Her assimilationist advocacy, however, left her open to criticism from contemporaries as well as those who followed her.

Fletcher, who died in 1923 at the age of 85, was a pioneering figure in anthropology and a woman of intense determination, strong opinions, and enormous observational skill.

Harriet Cosgrove

Harriet Cosgrove (1877-1970) became fascinated by the archaeology of the Southwest when she moved to Silver City, New Mexico, 1906. Silver City had been established near the ruins of pre-Columbian Mimbres culture which flourished from a.d. 200 to 1150. During the early years in New Mexico, Harriet, her husband, Burton, and son, Burton Jr,. spent much of their spare time exploring the Mimbres Valley.

In the 1920s the Cosgroves met A. V. Kidder who was Curator of North American Archaeology at the Peabody Museum and a key player in the burgeoning field of Southwestern archaeology. Kidder was impressed by the Cosgroves' amateur excavations and through his efforts the Cosgroves were hired by the Peabody Museum in 1924 to excavate the Swarts Ranch Ruin, a Classic Mimbres site (a.d. 1000-1150). Thus began a long-term association with Kidder and the Peabody Museum.

The work at Swarts established the Cosgroves among the elite of Southwestern archaeologists and reinforced their identity as a team. The work at Swarts was prodigious. Burton photographed the site. Harriet made pen and ink drawings of every bowl excavated and recorded every find in a series of field notes maintained for each season. The thoroughness of the field notes is astounding. Harriet described every room, its location, dimensions, and soil type. She recorded every artifact and described every burial. Published in 1932, the final report is still the primary reference for Mimbres scholars.

Their success at Swarts was a springboard to other work: they worked in the Gila River of New Mexico in 1928-1929 and in late 1929 with William H. Claflin Jr., of Belmont, Massachusetts at Stallings Island Mound in Columbia County, Georgia. Their next major project (1936-1939) was at the Hopi Pueblo of Awatovi in Arizona which was excavated under the direction of J. O. Brew (Director of the Peabody Museum from 1948-1967). Burton died during the first year of the project, but Harriet returned to Awatovi in 1937. She was in charge of the pottery tent for the duration of the Awatovi project and trained student and Indian assistants in washing, sorting, and cataloguing the artifacts.

Cora Du Bois

Cora Du Bois (1903-1991) was the first woman tenured in the Anthropology Department and the second woman ever be tenured in the Faculty of Arts and Sciences at Harvard University. She held the Zemurray-Stone Chair from 1954 to 1970, taught in the departments of Anthropology and Social Relations, and conducted research in California, Netherlands East Indies, and India. As a cultural anthropologist she made important contributions to culture and personality studies, the use of photography in analyzing field data, and interdisciplinary team research.

Like many other women anthropologists of her generation, her Ph.D. dissertation, which was concerned with girls' menstral rites in the New World, was based on library research. After completing her Ph.D. at Berkeley in 1932, Du Bois was unable to find an academic position, and worked as a teaching fellow and research assistant for the head of the Berkeley department, Alfred Kroeber, from 1932-1935. While working for Kroeber, Du Bois did salvage ethnography with the Wintu Indians in northern California and published on the Ghost Dance of 1870.

In 1935, Du Bois received a National Research Council Fellowship to investigate how psychiatric training might be used by professional anthropologists. With her fellowship, Du Bois returned to the east coast, spending six months at what was then the Boston Psychopathic Hospital, now the Murray Psychological Clinic, and six months with Abram Kardiner at the New York Psychoanalytic Society. In addition, Du Bois taught at Hunter College in 1936-1937 while formulating her goals for field research in Alor. From 1937-1939, Du Bois lived and conducted research on the remote island of Alor, part of the Netherlands East Indies, now Indonesia. In keeping with her focus on psychological anthropology, Du Bois administered Roscharch tests to the Alorese in the hopes of using these data to make systematic comparisons between cultures. Her research was designed to probe a basic Alorese personality structure, which, she believed, could be correlated with specific cultural institutions. The research resulted in a monograph, *The People of Alor*.

Like many anthropologists, Du Bois's academic research was interrupted by World War II. Du Bois joined the war effort as a member of the Office of Strategic Services working in the Research and Analysis Branch as Chief of the Indonesia section. In 1944 she moved from Washington, D.C., to Ceylon to head the Southeast Asia Command, for which she received the Exceptional Civilian Service Award in 1945. Among her duties were the running of resistance movements in Southeast Asian countries under Japanese occupation.

Du Bois worked for the State Department and the World Health Organization from 1946 until 1954-5 when she accepted the Zemurray-Stone Chair at Harvard University. The Zemurray-Stone Chair, which was established in 1947 by Samuel Zemurray in honor of his two children, Samuel, Jr. and Doris Zemurray-Stone, was a Radcliffe Chair to be given to the female academic of Harvard's choosing. Du Bois was the second recipient of the chair. While at Harvard Du Bois initiated a long-term research project on the Indian temple city of Bhubaneswar. During this research Du Bois oversaw the work and training of a number of Harvard graduate students involved in the Bhubaneswar project. In 1970 at the age of 67 Du Bois retired from Harvard, and from 1970-1975 took up a post as Professor-at-Large at Cornell University.

Cora Du Bois was a kind of anthropologist sojouner for 43 years of her long 59 year career-doing research, teaching, and government service. Throughout her jobs and travels, she also did anthropology: pioneering new approaches in interdisciplinary methodologies and culture-personality studies. She is often described as a formidable woman and a good friend-perhaps these designations carry some of the pride and passion that made up Du Bois's character.

IMPORTANCE OF FEMINISM IN ANTHROPOLOGY

Feminism has had a profound effect on anthropology as a discipline and on anthropological theory. This effect is evident in the changes made obvious since the advent of feminist work. Feminism began to take shape in the 1970s, where it began its long and arduous history. Many people cringe at the sound of the word feminism because it brings to mind images of women burning bras and "femi-Nazis" loudly protesting for equality. In the beginning, women knew they had to "expose sexism in public and private life, to alter the male-biased presumptions of scholarly and popular culture" (di Leonardo 1991: 2). This was quite a task to take on and so feminists are often viewed as having gone a bit too far.

The history of feminist work was brought on by the civil rights movements, anti-war sentiments, environmental and foreign policy concerns and gay and minority rights movements of the 1970s. American anthropology has always been about looking at ourselves by looking at others, this idea was not brought on by feminists. However, in the late Victorian era of Marx and Freud, evolutionary debates led to the belief that man had always dominated women. In 1965 the Brit Radcliffe-Brown postulated structural-functionalism as a theoretical framework. The American relocation and killing of the Native Americans prevented this framework from applying there. The Americans collected any information on their culture that they could get, thus emphasizing culture not society. American psychology was well established and American anthropologists were inclined "toward the psychological arena" and became the "culture and personality" theoretical learnings of the two most famous female anthropologists of the early twentieth century (di Leonardo 1991: 5). However influential these women were, they were still discriminated against. Margaret Mead and Ruth Benedict were students of Franz Boas and quite well known. Mead was famous for her writings of cross-cultural malleability of "natural" sex roles, but had never held an official department position and Benedict lost the chair position to a man when Boas retired.

In the 1970s anthropologists began looking at men's and women's different experiences as topics on their own terms. Before the 1970s, most theoretical movements ignored gender differences. However, prefeminist ethnographers gave rich information on gender. They would often take their wives on fieldwork expeditions and the women would write the women's point of view, which was either written into her husband's account or written independently (di Leonardo 1991: 6). Feminists began re-writing ethnographies, such as Malinowski's Trobriand Islands, to consider women's lives but in the process were also rewriting theory. Micaela di Leonardo states that Collier's and Lamphere's work on the dynamics of kinship and politics is a partial improvement on Radcliffe-Brown. Yanagisako also looked at symbolism in kinship which is a feminist twist on the cultural approach to kinship by David Shneider (di Leonardo 1991: 9).

Marilyn Strathern (1988) states that feminist scholarship organizes knowledge differently than most social sciences and challenges the way in which anthropology organizes knowledge (Strathern 1988: 23). She had previously stated that anthropology is a tolerant discipline that has many specializations and frameworks. Marxism, structuralism and symbolic anthropology all exist and this tolerance allowed for feminist ideas and the study of gender (Strathern 1987: 280). However, the tendency of anthropology to reduce feminism to one among many theories is countered by the idea that feminist activists might reduce anthropological knowledge of other cultures to little more than documentation of the different conditions in which women live. I believe feminism fits into anthropology well because all previous thought was from the point of view of men, thus only half the story was usually analyzed. Generalizations were made such as the Trobrianders do this... and the Trobrianders believe this... without the whole picture of what the women do and believe. The politics of feminism can be applied to anthropology, but theory and practice are causes of tension in the discipline. Feminist anthropology is not just about adding women to the picture, but instead about confronting the conceptual and analytical faults of disciplinary theory (Moore 1988: 4).

There are two types of feminism- radical feminism that attempts to change the basis of society and the assimilated feminism in academia, that views women in society and studies their point of view. Barrett states in Strathern (1988) that the ideas of radical feminism are mostly incompatible with, if not hostile to, those of Marxism and that one of its political projects has been to show how women have been betrayed by socialists and socialism (Strathern 1988: 25). Barrett believes that Marxist thought deals with class relations, labor processes and the state without regard to women's oppression.

In contrast, Micaela di Leonardo mentions the many British feminists who were influenced strongly by Marxist theory without using Marx or Engels for evolutionist grand theorizing. She states that these feminists looked at the lives of women in particular societies in terms of historical and political-economic contexts. Some of these women include Patricia Caplan, Janet Bujra and Kate Young of whom the latter contributed to *Of Marriage and the Market* (1981). This work shares the Marxist framework of other social scientists and historians in attempting to describe women's roles in the evolving global economy (di Leonardo 1991: 14). Di Leonardo then agrees with Strathern and goes on to say that Western feminist thought has moved away from the economic-historical considerations toward psychology. The two major factors limiting evolutionist Marxist explanations are the fact that it uses the Victorian anthropological comparative method, to consider contemporary cultures as living in history. The second factor is that the ethnographic record shows too many counterexamples to the Marx and Engels model of sexually egalitarian small-scale societies. Illustrating this point is the fact that too many women in small-scale societies experienced exploitation and oppression because of men within their societies to argue that Western contact is responsible for the unequal gender relations in foraging and horticultural societies (di Leonardo 1991: 15).

Donna Haraway mentions both the good and the bad of feminist Marxism. She says that Marxism does not deal with the issues of women properly. Humanistic Marxism has always been polluted by the structuring theory of domination of nature in the "self-construction of man" and how it historicized anything women did that did not earn a wage (Haraway 1988: 578). She also concedes that Marxism was still a good resource as an epistemological feminist thought that sought feminist doctrines of objective vision. The starting points of Marxism were useful for feminists to get to their own versions of theories without disempowering posivitisms and relativisms. Marxism also converges with another approach, "feminist empiricism", to get a theory of science that emphasizes legitimate meanings of objectivity. This approach is not a radical constructivism riddled with semiology and narratology (Haraway 1988: 579).

Fredrich Engels's book *The Origin of the Family, Private Property, and the State* (1884) is a text that tries to link the history of the family to the development of private property. A feminist debate ensued because of his ideas and he stated that the growth of male-owned private property and the development of monogamous families changed women's position in society and led to the 'world-historical defeat of the female sex'. He stated that before this 'defeat' societies around the world were egalitarian (Moore 1988: 46). Engels sees both sexes as equals that can own property and take part in political and economic activities. His ideas are very influential in Marxist and feminist analyses of the subordination of women. Thus the connection that Engels makes between women's subordination and private property means that he views women's inferior status as directly related to the fact that they do not own the means of production.

Moore mentions Karen Sacks as a Marxist anthropologist who is interested in the idea of women's universal subordination. She attempted to modify Engels's idea that women were subordinate because of the development of private property. She states that there is 'too much data showing that women are not the complete equals of men in most non-class societies lacking private property' (Sacks in Moore 1988: 33). Despite this valid argument, she agrees with Engels's position because it tells of the conditions under which women become subordinate to men and because it takes into account historical and ethnographic data that shows women did not always stand subordinate to men around the world. Sacks's position allows for the examination of women's varying positions in societies everywhere.

Another problem for feminist work is to explain why women's work is always underestimated. Their contributions to household income and unwaged labor go largely unnoticed. One of the reasons for this is the definition of 'work'. Every society can have a different definition of work and it is sometimes only referred to as having a job or a way to make money. Esther Boserup provided a comparative analysis of women's work, based on data from many societies in the book *Women's Role in Economic Development* (1970). She was able to show that it is not always men who provide the home with food, because in Africa the women do most of the cultivation. She contrasted African societies to those of Asia and explained the marked difference in women's roles as due to population density, landholding systems and technology (Moore 1988: 44). Boserup also mentioned the negative effects of colonialism and capitalism on women. She explains the underestimation of women's work as an 'ideological bias underlying statistical categories that tends to undervalue women's work, and that subsistence activities usually omitted in the statistics of production and income are largely women's work' (Boserup in Moore 1988: 44).

To discuss women's work means to understand the structure of the household. Anthropology is also able to make clear the relationship between the family and household in social and historical contexts. Anthropological research has long made clear the cross-cultural differences in kinship systems and living arrangements. The definitions of 'family' and household' are different in all societies and tend to go through stages. Despite the definitional problems, households are important in feminist studies because they organize a large part of women's domestic and reproductive labor. The way the household is structured affects women's lives, especially their access to labor and income. Ann Whitehead studied labor practices in a farming community in the Bawku district of north eastern Ghana (1981) and noted that women work for men, juniors work for seniors, the poor work for the rich and all these relationships form social relations through kinship, residence and patronage. Women are expected to work for the elder men of the household, but the men will only work for the women if they can exchange labor with them (Whitehead in Moore 1988: 58). This results in less acreage for women compared to that of men. She states that women have weaker claims to land in this agnatic society and thus profit less from their farms than do men.

Most of today's feminists are attempting to challenge the universal (or male) point of view- to change as well as understand different anthropological thought and theory. The problem with early feminists, and the reason people think of "femi-Nazis", is because they had originally set out to change the paradigm. The best shifts in thought tend to occur without trying, and only get noticed later. Another problem with the shift to genders studies, is that women in different cultures do not always feel like women in Western cultures. Western women can be concerned with equality, but its not a universal sentiment of women everywhere. Australian aboriginal women are not interested in all of the men's activities and have their own ceremonies and activities that cannot be touched by men. Differences and asymmetry in culture do not necessarily mean inequality and that the men dominate the women. Henrietta Moore (1988) states that even in more egalitarian societies (like the Australian aborigines) are usually not seen as such because researchers are not able to understand the equality because they view difference and asymmetry as inequality and hierarchy (Moore 1988: 2).

Feminist anthropology attempts to look at societies gender relations in terms of their cultural values and views. Lila Abu-Lughod's (1987) study of Bedouin women shed light on a subject that would never have been touched if it were not for feminist work. She was able to show how the complex workings of social power can be traced by the resistance the women displayed. She describes her argument as having been 'that we should learn to read in various local and everyday resistences the existence of a range of specific strategies and structures of power' (Abu-Lughod 1987: 332). Men studying the culture would never have been able to get such information about the resistance of the Bedouin women. Marilyn Strathern (1988) states that women's perspective is conceived in resistance to or in conflict with men's views (Strathern 1988: 23) and this is precisely why gender studies are important in analyzing many cultures. Feminist analysis is instrumental to a more autonomous view of power relations.

Abu-Lughod also noted the fact that the Bedouin women relied entirely on men for money. There were no job opportunities for women, so they were dependent on their husbands for spending money which they used to reward their wives or withhold it as a punishment. Moore mentions Westernization and the effect of international capitalism as a reason for the changing views of women in many societies. She stated that development and wage labor made women more dependent on men by undermining traditional systems where women have had a certain amount of control over production and reproduction (Moore 1988: 33).

Another useful theory brought about by feminist work is one posed by Sherry Ortner whom began an important framework for studying the power of women through gender symbolism. She wrote an early article sorting through the problem of women's universal subordination as sexual asymmetry of cultural ideologies and symbols. She decided that women everywhere must be associated with something that every culture devalues. She concluded that it was ' "nature" in the most generalized sense' (Ortner 1974: 72). All cultures make the distinction between nature and human society in which culture attempts to transcend and control nature. Culture is superior to nature and Ortner says that women are associated with nature and men with culture thus, women should also be controlled and contained. This is a very important statement to make in feminist anthropology and she uses two general arguments to apply it to all cultures. First, women have reproduction functions and are closer to nature. Men seek cultural means of creation through technology while women are able to naturally reproduce through giving birth.

Secondly, since women have reproducing abilities they are limited to certain social functions which are seen as closer to nature, or the domestic domain. Women need to rear children and are associated with the pre-social or not yet culturally created person. Ortner says that children are associated with nature in a number of societies (Ortner 1974: 78). This also implies that women are mainly associated with the household while men operate in the public and political domain, thus are the ones identified with society. Ortner stresses that in reality women are not any closer to nature than men, she just identifies this as the cultural ideas that make women appear to be closer to nature in societies. Thus formulation of 'nature is to culture as female is to male' gave anthropology an analytical framework which had great impact in the late 1970s and early 1980s (Moore 1988: 15).

Of course there are criticisms to every new model imposed by anthropologists, and Strathern argues against Ortner's theory. She states that the demeaning value of domestic work is a Western construct and is not a cross-cultural representation of the domestic sphere, or even that of women.

Many societies do make a connection between 'female' and 'domestic', but Strathern states that these associations cannot be explained in terms of Western constructs such as nature/ culture and domestic/public (Strathern in Moore 1988: 40).

Questioning the cultural constructions of self through gender identity is where feminist anthropology continues to make an impact on theoretical development within the discipline. Annette Weiner re-analyzed Trobriand society to get the women's perspective and view women as individuals. She writes that women have considerable power within their domain and certain cultural activities are the domain of women alone. She emphasizes the fact that women should be viewed as persons. Daryl Feil studied the Enga of New Guinea and states that for women to be viewed as persons they need to participate in the socio-political activities that are in the domain of men which is in contrast to Sacks's idea that women have domains that are equal in value to those of men. Feil and Sacks differ again when Feil states that women's power lies in their day-to-day affairs and Weiner emphasizes the cultural power of the symbolic encoding of femaleness, evident in activities and objects which are specifically female (Moore 1988: 39). The question here is whether it is enough to say women are powerful in their own domains or must feminists argue that women have power in everyday social life in the public and political domains which are the domains of men. This is a problem that feminist anthropologists have been attempting to deal with in their studies.

In conclusion, the most important contribution feminist anthropology has made to the discipline was the development of theories relating to gender identity and the cultural construction of gender, and what it means to be a 'woman' (Moore 1988: 187). The advent of feminist work brought about the invention of the 'anthropology of gender', an important field of research that owes its existence to feminist anthropology. Feminist anthropology's most distinctive contribution is through demonstrating why an understanding of gender relations is important to the analysis of key questions in anthropology and in the social sciences as a whole. Feminist anthropology has made a comparative analysis of the cultural construction of gender, sexual division of labor, and the problems of capitalism. This comparative approach has allowed feminist anthropology to greatly advance the knowledge of these areas theoretically and empirically (Moore 1988: 195-196). Moore also states that the centrality that anthropology gives to the study of kinship relations in the context of the modern state suggests that feminist anthropology has an important contribution to make in the ways in which existing kinship systems structure state responses to the 'family' and the 'household'.

The feminist critique of the social sciences has been attributed to the breaking down of discipline barriers and the move towards multi-disciplinary scholarship. Feminist studies attempt not only to radicalize the disciplines, but to develop new research procedures and new relationships between academic theory and practice. Feminist anthropology emphasizes the relationship of gender differences to other forms of difference, which allows an opportunity to question the primacy which social anthropology has always accorded to cultural difference (Moore 1988: 1996). This is to suggest that forms of difference in human social life such as gender, class, race, culture, etc., are always experienced, constructed and mediated in interrelation with each other.

2

Anthropology
Feminist Interventions

The first intervention of feminist anthropologists into the field of kinship studies and, thence, into anthropology more generally, consisted in the creation of a discursive object that would permit the simultaneous critique of existing theories and the reassessment of its empirical claims. That category was "gender," understood as "the constitutive element of social relationships based on perceived differences between the sexes" and as "a primary way of signifying relationships of power". Indeed "power and difference" became the crucial axes of gender analysis from the 1980s onward.

Feminists began by accusing early social theorists, but perhaps especially Claude Lévi-Strauss, of mistaking an ideological justification for the oppression of women with an ontology of the social. Because women are treated as commodities does not imply that their functioning as commodities is logically intrinsic to social life everywhere. Because women are frequently relegated to private or domestic domains does not mean that the social world is logically bifurcated along the axis of public and private or that these domains would have to be gendered when they were. And because sexual difference is the primary structure for differentiation of labor and structuring power in small-scale societies that lack a public sphere does not mean that, logically, gender must be a salient structural principle only in domestic spheres when these are encompassed by larger public ones.

From these logical arguments emerged a series of questions regarding the universality and extremity of male dominance, the organization of domestic and public or political life, the relationship between political complexity and the status of women, the range of property systems through which women do or do not gain access to economic resources, and the more subterranean forms of power, value, renown, and influence that women exercise even in those contexts where formal authority is vested in male subjects. In essence, these questions and the energetic research that they spurred were driven by the pursuit of a counterexample. Evidence of equality or a different organizational imperative in one society would undermine claims for the universal virtue, necessity, or naturalness of particular inequalities everywhere else. Or so a generation of feminist scholars hoped. Their project was empiricist and comparativist, collaborative and emphatically political. Its result can be seen in the series of volumes they generated, including those edited by Michelle Rosaldo and Louise Lamphere (1974), Rayna Reiter (1975), Carol MacCormack and Marilyn Strathern (1980), Mona Etienne and Eleanor Leacock (1980), and Sherry Ortner and Harriett Whitehead (1981).

The contributors to these volumes arrived at various and oftentimes contradictory conclusions. Some of the writers included in Rosaldo and Lamphere's collection, notably Rosaldo, Nancy Chodorow, and Ortner, concluded that male dominance *is* universal, with Rosaldo attributing it to the division of labor and the distribution of authority across a violently enforced private/public divide, Chodorow locating women's exclusion from the public in their maternal function and the socialization of girls, and Ortner revising Lévi-Strauss's argument to claim that women are universally perceived as relatively close to nature and therefore thought to be in need of more vigorous regulatory oversight. Other writers, however, especially those influenced by Marxist thought and Friedrich Engels's *The Origin of the Family, Private Property, and the State,* differed. Karen Sacks and, later, Eleanor Leacock (1981) argued that not all societies are dominated by men and that egalitarianism prevails in those where private property, and the particular construction of women as private property, has not yet developed. In this case male dominance is a function of history and a relatively recent emergence. Still others, such as Peggy Sanday, asserted that male dominance is vitiated over time as technology and the transformation of production attenuates the advantages conferred by physical strength.

Such arguments stood or failed according to the persuasiveness with which the ethnographic evidence was adduced, and many of the writers later recanted or were persuaded by competing positions. One of the most lucid and sustained theoretical critiques to emerge from Rosaldo and Lamphere's 1974 volume was penned by Gayle Rubin under the title "The Traffic in Women: Notes Toward a 'Political Economy' of Sex." Rubin's essay commenced with a new category, that of the "sex/gender system." It was intended to overcome the prevalent dichotomy between sexual and economic systems and to prevent sexual relations from being reduced to reproductive function. As a formally empty category, the idea of a sex/gender system demanded ethnographic specification of the same sort that would distinguish between socialist or capitalist production. Rubin took Lévi-Strauss to task precisely for his lack of such differentiation, especially on the question of the traffic in women. Failing to differentiate between historically actual cases of women who are "given in marriage, taken in battle, exchanged for favors, sent as tribute, traded, bought and sold" rendered the notion vacuous for Rubin, and she observed that men are also trafficked - for different purposes. Michael Peletz would corroborate this assertion in 1996 with descriptions of the traffic in men by women in nineteenth-century Malay communities.

It is, however, in her deconstruction of the concept of gender, as assumed in Lévi-Strauss's *The Elementary Structures of Kinship,* that Rubin made her most incisive intervention. Observing that the incest taboo as described by Lévi-Strauss is not merely a prohibition on incest but also on homosexuality and on sameness, one that orchestrates desire in terms of sexual difference, Rubin offered as counterexamples those instances in which same-sex relations are considered necessary for the production of adult gender (as in some parts of New Guinea) and those in which same-sex marriage is permitted (as among the Azande or the Dahomey), or where institutionalized transvestism is practiced (such as Native North America or India). Given these facts, she asserted, the taboo is not universal but merely the representation of a particular, if commonplace, ideology - for which, she admits, both Freud and Lévi-Strauss offer refined descriptions and unapologetic but illegitimate justifications.

ANTHROPOLOGY AND WOMANIST THEORY

Anthropology is an ambitious science which, from its earliest origins, has sought to answer questions about the infinite complexities of the human experience. While scholars often trace the origins of the discipline to the Greek philosopher, Herodotus (5th century B. C.), there is evidence that every group of people (including those who would become the "primitive" subjects of anthropological inquiry) has questioned the human condition and sought to derive explanations for human behavior and human purpose. Thinkers from every group of existing people have sought to understand the meaning of human constructs such as kinship, war, migration, social structure, and political organization. Further, anthropological explanations of the human condition by non-literate people have been expressed through art, mythology, religious practices, ceremonial displays, and, of course, through the oral tradition.

The formalization of anthropology as a scientific discipline in the late nineteenth century meant that the observations, hypotheses, and theories of "the study of man" were generated from and based upon that which we now call empirical data. Such data gained great respectability over so-called "superstitions" as people of the Western world became influenced by rationalist thinking during the eighteenth century's Age of Enlightenment. As the discipline developed, a number of plausible - if not problematic - theories traversed the anthropological terrain, exerting various degrees of influence and inciting further theorizing from proponents and critics alike.

Thus, anthropology has been shaped and influenced by such diverse theoretical perspectives as evolutionism, historical particularism, structural-functionalism, cultural materialism, and Marxism. Additionally, there are the paradigms of psychological anthropology, symbolic anthropology, and structuralism. This wealth of theories has led some scholars to label anthropologists as eclectics: that is, as scientists who are unable to commit to any particular epistemological or theoretical principles (Harris, 1979). Murphy describes the lack of a dominant theory by defining anthropology as "a pluralistic discipline that loosely shelters a plethora of interest and which lacks a center".

Despite scholarly critiques of the state of anthropological theory, the anthropological project is a fundamentally discursive one whose task is the production of knowledge on every aspect of culture. Harrison (1995b) has referred to anthropology as the most interdisciplinary of all social sciences. However, in both theory and application, anthropology continues to replicate the model of the (white) scholar venturing into Third World communities1 to observe, probe, interpret, and change. Critiques of anthropology's colonialist and imperialist implications have been numerous (Asad, 1975; Drake, 1980; Harrison, 1991; Huizer and Mannheim, 1979; and Hymes, 1972, among others).

Nevertheless, anthropologists who are members of oppressed groups are attracted to the discipline because of our "growing understanding that rigorous analysis and documentation of the cultures and histories of our peoples can be essential tools in the quest for progressive social change" (Gordon, 1991). Feminist and womanist theorists also have critically examined the discipline's historical connections to hegemonic systems as well as its value in knowledge production and representation. For example, Mohanty contends that anthropology "is an example of disciplinary knowledge which signifies the power of naming and the contests over meaning of definitions of the self and other".

As such, anthropology has the potential of being a crucial tool for struggle and resistance. Harrison argues for a reconsideration of anthropology's multiple knowledges (especially that knowledge created by anthropologists of color) and a recognition of the "silences and subjugations that influence the discipline's development". In another scholarly essay, Harrison identifies the invisibility and silences of women of color in the anthropological canon and concludes: "In the process of redefining anthropology's critical project(s) and of reconstituting anthropological authority, we must offset the persistent pattern of relegating the work of women - and that of women of color in particular - to the discipline's periphery".

In the tradition of those womanist scholars who have sought to broaden the meaning of feminism and of those anthropologists whose work examines the interlocking hierarchies of gender, race, and class as well as the subjugated knowledges and alternative methodologies of anthropology (Bolles, 1987; Harrison, 1995b; Mikell, 1982; Steady, 1981), I began exploring the implications and challenges of identifying and articulating a womanist voice in anthropology. As a graduate student, my womanist perspective was subsumed by the discipline itself. Recognizing the centrality and the authority of whiteness and maleness in the discipline, I struggled with my own questions about the roles of people of color as creators of knowledge in anthropology. Further, Black women's presence in anthropology (as the focus of research or as researchers) was virtually unrecognized in my program of study. Consequently, my development as a potential contributor to anthropological scholarship involved a conscious process of independently seeking out radical and alternative knowledge.

Now, as a scholar with some intellectual freedom, I seek to participate in the paving of a path for myself and others who would define themselves as womanists. This path is paved with womanist ideas on Black women as scholars, researchers, leaders, and active creators of culture and communities. I define womanist ideas as those informed by the interaction of Afrocentric, multicultural, and feminist theoretical interpretations of political, economic, historical, social, and cultural phenomena. According to Collins (1991), the foundation of womanist thought consists of specialized knowledge created by women of the African diaspora which clarifies a standpoint of and for Black women. That standpoint consists of "the experiences and ideas shared by [Black] women that provide a unique angle of vision on self, community, and society". Womanist thought is informed by the legacies of awareness, activism, intellectualism, struggle, and self-definition of women of Africa and its diaspora.

Yet, what does it mean to be a womanist anthropologist? How does one define, create, and operationalize womanist theory in anthropology? In the following discussion, I will address these questions by describing some of the ways in which womanist theory can inform teaching and research in cultural anthropology. I argue that womanist theory in anthropological pedagogy and research is congruent with a relevant, holistic, and humanistic anthropology. As a womanist, I am professionally, politically, and personally concerned that the discipline of anthropology is one that embraces the multiple cultural interactions of all women of color, especially women of Africa and its diaspora.

ANTHROPOLOGICAL IMAGES OF BLACK WOMEN

Regardless of sexual affiliation, a researcher cannot really escape the ideological and cultural influences that are contributory factors in the formulation of concepts, values, orientations, and methodologies.

- Filomena Chioma Steady, The Black Woman Cross-Culturally

Historically, Black women have been represented in anthropological and related social science research in a number of ways that appear to be authoritatively or empirically based.

These representations include: Black women as the exotic, primitively sexual Other; Black women as the dysfunctional or pathological Other; or Black women as the invisible, passive Other. To emphasize the notion of Black women as the exotic, primitively sexual Other, Black women's bodies were examined and displayed in the name of science. Giddings (1994) cites the degrading treatment of Sarah Bartmann (1790-1815), a South African woman, who in 1810 was publicly exhibited in London. Fascinated with the size and structure of Bartmann's buttocks, European scientists displayed her for five years until she died in Paris at age twenty-five. As the dysfunctional or pathological Other, Black women have been portrayed by sociologists as the domineering matriarch, solely responsible for the demise of the Black family. As the invisible, passive Other, Black women's creative and complex contributions to culture in Africa and the Americas were ignored.

In more benign representations, Black women have been included among the oppressed without deep considerations of the interlocking hierarchies that affect Black women's lives. It only has been in the mid-twentieth century that Black women in social science research have become active as scholars attempting to document liberatory and humanistic data on lives of women of Africa and its diaspora.

The purpose of this discussion is to introduce some general observations on the ways in which Black women have been represented in the research of these two groups of anthropologists. The examination of the early works of the structural-functionalists and feminist anthropologists because these represent two periods in which anthropologists were generating new questions, exploring new theories, and feeling quite free in expressing their interpretations. Second, these two groups were selected because of their anthropological foci: A significant body of anthropological literature on Africa came from the British structural-functionalists, and a significant body of work on women came from feminist anthropologists. Black women are a part of both of these extensively examined populations.

Finally, these groups were selected because of the distinctive historical and political time periods in which these anthropologists developed theories. It is important to understand that in every historical period, scientific inquiry is influenced by the state of the larger world capitalist system (as well as by attempts to challenge the systems of Dower). Historically, this capitalist ideology has depended upon the free or low wage labor of Black women and other people of color, while simultaneously denying and devaluing the contributions of these same people. Since politics, economics, scientific inquiry, and knowledge are intricately interconnected, this devaluation of nonwhite people is sometimes reflected in social science research. Anthropology has been no exception.

Although misrepresented, Black women were a critical foundation of early anthropological inquiry. Steady (1981) argues that long before the advent of a feminist focus on women, Black (African) women had been the undefined or unacknowledged Other: "It can even be claimed that to some extent she was used, directly or indirectly, as a guinea pig for the development of a significant body of anthropological theory in Africa and sociological theory in the United States and in the Caribbean".

The use of the Black woman indirectly is illustrated in early British anthropology. Using structural-functionalism as a theoretical framework, British anthropologists attempted to make sense of living societies by adopting an organic analogy. That is, institutions such as kinship, religion, politics, and economics interacted with each other in the same way that organs of the human body interact (Radcliffe-Brown, 1965). These scientists believed that the components of a social system had specific purposes that maintained the integrity and stability of the entire system (Lett, 1987). One edited text consisting of detailed descriptions of the social structures of eight African societies was produced by Fortes and Evans-Pritchard (1940). In the same paradigmatic tradition, Middleton and Tait (1958) produced a text that included six studies of "the reciprocal relations between descent groups and local political groups, between lineages and clans and local and political communities".

One example of African women's invisibility or misrepresentation is taken from Bohannan's chapter in the Middleton and Tait text. Bohannan describes the social organization of the Tiv, a tribe in Northern Nigeria. The chapter is an excellently detailed description of geography, language, housing compounds, genealogy, political structure, warfare, leadership patterns, and the maintenance of peace and order. Based on Bohannan's narrative, men were her only informants and women were mentioned in passing only as the bearers of men's children.

African women's centrality to various forms of human organization (as maintainers of economic systems; as producers of food, social order, children, culture; as partners in leadership with men) is not apparent in the ethnographic descriptions of any of the fourteen studies of the aforementioned texts. In their zeal to develop scholarship on so-called "primitive" or "simple" cultures in Africa and in their quest to be among the first to categorize these systems for the literate world, these anthropologists assumed that men were the key actors in the creation and maintenance of social structure. Even when African women's presence was acknowledged, their contributions remained peripheral. Further, these anthropologists worked assiduously to describe African political systems even as these systems were being destroyed by colonialism and imperialism.

Yet, it would not have served the economic and political progress of their country for the structural-functionalists to acknowledge the destruction of African political institutions by European colonizers. It would not have served the scientific aims of these anthropologists to determine how the colonial era was disrupting the lives of women as well as men. It would later be determined that African women suffered tremendously from colonialist and imperialist changes, "for after having had a role in traditional forms of organization, under colonialism they discovered themselves systematically excluded from any participation in the new set-up".

The success of early anthropological research in Africa owes much to the European expansionist ideology of the fifteenth century. This forceful and violent expansion which stimulated the practice and business of transatlantic slave trading) followed by white rule of various African countries, opened up the continent to the very curious eyes of those who wanted to compare European culture to that of primitive or simple societies. Willis contends that anthropology's formalization in the later nineteenth century "coincided with the shift from 'booty' colonialism to imperialism, which stressed profit from the control, exploitation, and preservation of cheap colored workers and consumers". While these early European anthropologists were strongly influenced by the structural-functionalist paradigm, they also were influenced by an increasingly imperialistic ideology that was working to the advantage of European countries. Further, these anthropologists set off on their adventurous explorations of Africa with the unchallenged assumption that universally, whether in complex or so-called simple societies, males were dominant, militaristic, necessarily oppressive, possessed of the most coveted positions in those tasks associated with the division of labor, and ascribed the rightful policymakers in their own particular hierarchies.

Much later in social science history, the feminist anthropology of the 1970s emerged. As di Leonardo explains, "The political source of feminist scholarship, early 1970s feminism, was not the first but the second major wave of women's rights thought and activism" (1991). As a relatively homogeneous group (white female scholars), Western feminist anthropologists of the 1970s sought to "expose sexism in public and private life, and to alter the male-biased presumptions of scholarly and popular culture" (di Leonardo). Similar to their non-feminist anthropological predecessors, these anthropologists believed that universal male domination did exist as a cultural phenomenon. However, feminist anthropologists sought to identify this domination and explain its manifestations, as well as its political, economic, and social impacts on women. Informed primarily by Western women's political, social, and economic issues, feminist anthropologists developed theories on universal sexual asymmetry (Rosaldo, 1974).

Some feminist anthropologists such as Ortner (1974) argued that women's subjugation by men was a universal phenomenon because of women's association with nature. Rosaldo (1974) attributed universal male dominance to a dichotomy between the domestic sphere, which associated women with nurturing, homemaking, and related activities, and the public sphere, which has been viewed as the male domain in societies.

Another similarity that feminist anthropologists shared with the British structural-functionalists was in their mutual fascination with nonwhite people as the subjects of their scientific curiosity. Yet it is true that this fascination is anthropology's legacy: "To a considerable extent, anthropology has been the social science that studies dominated colored peoples - and their ancestors - living outside the boundaries of modern white society" (Willis, 1972). Feminist anthropologists were strongly committed to the comparative method in order to prove universals or to explain common themes across cultures in women's lives. In the anthropological tradition (inspired by evolutionist theory), feminist anthropologists compared the beliefs and practices of women who anthropologists felt represented simplified versions of Western culture.

As just one example, in a 1974 essay, Tanner compared the roles of women in kinship systems among Indonesians, Africans, and African Americans (Tanner, 1974). Focusing on the concept of matrifocality (the structural centrality of mother roles within a kinship system), Tanner concluded that there are social, economic, and cultural factors that determine this phenomenon. She also concluded that women's centrality in kinship systems among the Javanese, the Atjehnese, the Minangkabau, the Igbo, and among African Americans is not an indicator of pathology or marginality. However, do African-American women have to be compared with women of different cultures in order to refute the myth of a Black matriarchy? How does one compare kinship systems of Black Americans across the United States with ethnic groups residing at the northern tip of Sumatra or even in eastern Nigeria?

Similar questions surround the early feminist literature on women of color. One problem was that feminist anthropologists were so consumed with asserting themselves (in a very sexist, male-dominated discipline) and with changing anthropology, that their universals became generalizations. Black women and other women of color were no longer invisible; but, inadvertently, their lives were made to seem simplistic. While Western feminist theorists posed ideas that served to legitimize the study of gender and focus the blurred images of women in the anthropological picture, African women anthropologists developed scholarship in a womanist inspired tradition. That scholarship was developed without exploitation or use of the comparative method. African womanist anthropologists examined their own cultures for the inherent truths and realities that are evident to one who is both native and scientific observer. Even today, African anthropologists are challenging Western feminist assumptions.

First, African womanists have contributed to the anthropological literature by describing the communal structure of traditional African societies which assumed egalitarian interactions among African women and men. They also have shown that in some traditional African societies, certain politico-religious roles are gender-determined (Okonjo, 1981). Second, African womanists have shown that a close connection with nature served neither to subordinate nor to heighten women's status in traditional African societies, since the rhythms of African life were guided by nature. Thus, the problematic nature/culture dichotomy did not manifest itself in traditional African life as it did (and still does) in Western culture. Ultimately, colonialism, imperialism, and their legacies continue to be the primary oppressors of African women, argues Steady (1993). Discussions of the experiences of the majority of African women must focus on multiple forms of oppression, not simply sexual asymmetry.

This brief discussion of the early work of structural-functionalists and feminist anthropologists has been purposely narrow. Indeed, there are many laudable insights from and enlightening dimensions to the research and theories of these scholars. Moreover, anthropology has changed significantly since its formalization in the late nineteenth century, and it continues to evolve as the human experience changes. Structural-functionalism outgrew its usefulness as a theoretical analysis because it did not address the inevitable impact of change on societies. Western feminists are still firmly developing a place in anthropology as they reexamine their assumptions about the universality of the female experience. Further, the anthropological literature on ethnicity, women, and gender has matured considerably. Although not widely recognized, some of these changes can be attributed to womanist epistemology.

A Womanist Epistemological Framework in Anthropology

We must act with deliberation and commitment in order to ensure that all women have a voice and an audience for the telling of their lives.

-Gwendolyn Etter-Lewis, Black Women's Life Stories

A significant aspect of womanist epistemology is understanding the ways in which Black women's lives are affected by many complex interlocking hierarchies, including "slavery, imperialism, colonialism, neocolonialism, poverty, racism and apartheid" (Steady, 1993). Another aspect of womanist epistemology is the awareness and analysis of stereotypes and images of Black womanhood that justify and perpetuate these forms of oppression. Womanist epistemology also is influenced by a need to elucidate the multiple roles that Black women play in the struggle for the survival of the Black community and in the struggle for institutional change (Collins, 1991). Theorizing by womanist thinkers is a way of speaking out and shedding light on these hierarchies, stereotypes, and negative images, while simultaneously acknowledging Black women as capable contributors to humanity. James contends that womanist theorizing emerges from Black women's experiences with racism, ethnocentrism, sexism, homophobia, and classism. Moreover, womanist theorizing is transformative for Black women and their communities, even as Black women challenge their own communities to eliminate oppressive beliefs and practices (James, 1993).

Yet, before addressing the significance of a womanist epistemological framework in anthropology, it is necessary to clarify terminology. One of the problems with the term "feminism," as political identity, is that Black women generally associate feminist analyses and politics with white women, who, along with white men, are benefactors of systemic racism. In response to this term, "womanist," "Black feminist," "African feminist," and "Third World feminist" have been used in a number of contexts to denote the liberatory theories, perspectives, and actions of Black women who are particularly concerned with Black women's historical, cultural, social, economic, and political realities globally. These terms are used to address a feminism that often has been characterized as "liberal, bourgeois, or reformist with a narrow conception of feminist terrain as an almost singularly antisexist struggle" (Johnson-Odim, 1991). For Black women activists and scholars, there is an ongoing challenge to develop a lexicon that describes an autonomous, relevant, humanistic, and community-focused epistemology.

The development and use of unique and culturally grounded terminology does not distract from the larger issues involved in Black women's liberatory work. Rather, the use of the term "womanist" clarifies our connection and commitment to understanding our own cultural realities as Black women. Thus, Walker's (1983) spirited and succinct definition of the word is more than just a response to the narrowness of traditional feminist ideas. The word derives from "womanish," a term used by Black women to describe the boldness of some Black girls. Politically, a womanist is one who calls attention to the multiple oppression of Black women, but also is committed to the survival of all people. A womanist understands that the well-being of her own folk is related to the larger struggle of the human community (Walker, 1983).

Womanist anthropologists are reconceptualizing feminist ideas and identifying the centrality of the feminine in African and African diasporan culture. For example, as an anthropologist and native of Sierra Leone, Steady (1987) argues that there is an "African feminism" which she defines on two complementary levels. On one level, African feminism is a traditional way of knowing that is embedded in African life. Thus, in pre-colonial African societies, the dominant ideology of group survival dictated balance and egalitarianism: "Men and women in traditional African societies had spheres of autonomy - in economic, social, ritual, and political terms - ensured by various mechanisms of checks and balances" (Steady, 1987). Women's importance in all aspects of African life was understood. Steady's arguments are supported by Aidoo (1981), Okonjo (1981), and Sudarkasa (1987), each of whom provides detailed historic or ethnographic descriptions of women's roles in African societies.

On another level, Steady defines African feminism as Black women's awareness of multiple oppression in post-colonial Africa. Black women researchers, in particular, operationalize African feminist (or womanist) thinking by developing liberatory scholarship on Black women in Africa and its diaspora and by counteracting the destructive impact of research that has been used to dominate Black people (Steady, 1987). Collins (1991) argues that because knowledge has been defined by white male scholars, thinkers, and institutions, womanist ways of knowing have been suppressed, distorted, and silenced. Thus, in intellectual domains, womanist knowledge is subjugated knowledge (Collins, 1991). While womanist knowledge has been subjugated in all of the social sciences, this subjugation particularly has been evident in anthropology. In addressing anthropology's historical relationship with Black people, Drake contends that at the turn of the century, African-American intellectuals considered anthropology to be their enemy, "much as African intellectuals have tended to consider the discipline an adjunct to oppressive colonialism" (Drake, 1980). Thus, until the early 1920s, there were no Black scholars in anthropology. Blacks everywhere were viewed not as creators of knowledge, but as subjects for the advancement of ethnographies and research careers. Further, we know that Black women's lives were distorted, minimized, or rendered invisible by anthropology.

How then, can one argue for the development of a womanist voice in anthropology? First, to contend that there is a womanist intellectual tradition in anthropology. This tradition was created by the first Black women who dared to claim anthropology as their discipline and whose work contributed to the idea that this discipline could be changed. Second, to argue that there are contemporary scholars of anthropology who have legitimized the concept of native anthropology and whose work I implemented in a liberatory (i.e., womanist) tradition. I will now expand upon each of these points.

Although never attaching themselves to the descriptor "womanist," the first Black women anthropologists represent womanist ways of thinking and knowing in their research interests, methodologies, and interpretations. When we seek out the work of the Black foremothers of anthropology, we reclaim a Black women's intellectual tradition which consists of expansive and explosive concepts and ideas on all aspects of humanity. The reclaiming of this tradition means moving beyond what has been offered in traditional academic discourse and rediscovering the works of extraordinary Black women thinkers. In anthropology, this rediscovery entails examining Black women's research and ethnographic work as well as exploring the thoughts of Black women not previously considered to be intellectuals (or even real anthropologists).

Of great relevance to the professional development of womanist anthropologists is the exploration and examination of the works and lives of the women who began the foundation of a Black women's intellectual tradition in anthropology. Drake (1980) cites Caroline Bond Day (1889-

1948) as possibly the first African American to achieve a Ph.D. in anthropology. During a time in which white citizens were consumed with fears about the evils of miscegenation, Day produced genealogical data on interracial families in America. Working within the climate of a racially divided society that was driven by a need to categorize Blacks based on skin color, Day's research, entitled A Study of Some Negro-White Families in the United States (1932), revealed kinship ties between Blacks and prominent Southern white families. Harrison (1995a) contends that Day's work contributed to the developing antiracist research in anthropology by refuting notions of the degenerative effects of interracial offspring.

Little is known about the responses to her work during the time of its publication. It would be fascinating to have access to any reactions to Day's research by Black leaders and thinkers such as Du Bois (1868-1963) and Garvey (1887-1940), who wrote and spoke about color issues in the Black community. However, it is interesting to note that Day provided an intellectual perspective on a topic that continues to influence relationships in American society even into the latter part of the twentieth century.

The usefulness of Day's research in illuminating the culture of that anomalous minority known as free Blacks during the antebellum period probably has not been explored to its fullest extent. It certainly has not been utilized in traditional anthropological pedagogy. Yet, as recently as 1991, Day's 1932 research was cited in Ambiguous Lives: Free Women of Color in Rural Georgia, 1789-1879 (Alexander, 1991). Despite her contributions to physical anthropology, very little is known about this scholar and her self-determined struggles to become an anthropologist during the Jim Crow era.

Somewhat more is known about the struggles and self-determination of another Black woman who came to anthropology shortly after the publication of Day's research. What we know of this woman primarily occurs through the study of her novels, short stories, and folklore collections. Of this woman, Drake writes:

It was hard for those who knew her after she was a success to visualize Zora Neale Hurston submitting to the pedestrian humdrum grind involved in getting a Ph.D. She didn't. But she must have played the academic game to some extent because Langston Hughes once remarked that Zora was the only person on earth who could have gone up and down the streets of Harlem as she did, with her strange instruments, actually persuading people to let her measure their skulls and lips. . . . (1980)

Despite her very successful resistance to the "humdrum" of academia, Hurston's vibrant creativity, her fascination with the humanity of poor southern Blacks, and her unconventional analysis and presentation of Black English, made unprecedented contributions to the cultural and linguistic anthropology of the Black South. Emerging feminist scholars such as Visweswaran (1994) argue that Hurston's work is one of the ignored classics of the anthropological canon, and should be examined by anthropologists for its ethnographic value.

However, Hurston's ethnography continues to be unrecognized in traditional anthropological pedagogy. It is critical, however, that those seeking to create a womanist vision in anthropology know of Hurston's uses of anthropology. Further, it is of consequence that womanist anthropologists become familiar with the impact of anthropological training on Black women like Day, Hurston (1891-1960), Katherine Dunham, Ellen Irene Diggs, and Vera Mae Green. Certainly, these women may not have called themselves Black feminist or womanist thinkers, yet they were indeed revolutionary in choosing nontraditional paths for their professional lives. The choices made by these nontraditional scholars form the foundation of a Black women's intellectual tradition in anthropology.

The work of contemporary Black women anthropologists also supports the idea of a womanist voice in this discipline. Black women's work in anthropology is characterized by diversity in subject matter (including works that advance alternative methodologies and experimental writing, works that represent analyses of educational systems, and works that represent political economy and class analyses); by ongoing theoretical analyses of gender, race, and class issues; and by an understanding of the potential liberatory value of anthropology. More important, womanist anthropologists strive to transform the discipline by acknowledging a Black women's intellectual tradition and addressing the marginalization of Black women's scholarship in anthropology. For example, in response to those who dismiss Hurston's anthropological endeavors, Mikell (1982, 1983) shows that Hurston's anthropological training influenced and enhanced her ability to portray the distinctive culture of rural Black people.

Womanist anthropologists also explore the contributions of womanist interlocutors to anthropology. Thus, Harrison (1995b) analyzes Walker's connections to anthropology not only because of Walker's rediscovery of Hurston's work, but also because of Walker's novel, The Temple of My Familiar (1989), "which should be seen as an integral part of the broader literature on the politics of representing gender, race, and cultural history" (Harrison, 1995b).

The anthropological idea challenges the researcher to observe, ask questions, and document various realities from the perspectives of those who live those realities. Womanist anthropology brings a unique and very necessary dimension to the discipline in several ways. First, by exploring and recording the cultural interactions of Black women and the Black community, womanist anthropologists counter charges that one cannot effectively study one's own people. In the tradition of Zora Neale Hurston, womanist anthropologists believe that "the best researcher [is] one who [has] an element of commonality with the people being studied" (Mikell, 1982). Second, while critiquing anthropology's colonialist history, womanist anthropologists move beyond the critique and seek to transform anthropology by introducing new subject matter, implementing alternative methodologies, and refusing to be relegated to a peripheral space in the discipline. Third, through research, womanist anthropologists challenge the images of Black womanhood that have been created by social science in order to control Black women politically and economically. This is done by asserting Black women as legitimate subjects of study, by identifying the multiple oppressive forces in Black women's lives, and by creating a space for the visible representation of Black women as active participants in the creation of culture, knowledge, and power.

WOMANIST THEORY IN ANTHROPOLOGICAL PEDAGOGY AND RESEARCH

Collins (1991) has developed and articulated a womanist epistemological framework that defines some of the key elements of womanist theory. These elements of womanist theory can serve as principles for the development of sound social science research, and have strengthened my development as an anthropologist. Among the principles that compose the foundation of womanist theory is a "recurring humanist vision" (Collins, 1991) which speaks to autonomy rather than separatism and a commitment to the survival and wholeness of all people. The nineteenth-century Black feminist thinker Anna Julia Cooper (1859-1964) expressed this humanist vision in an 1893 speech in which she declared, "We take our stand on the solidarity of humanity, the oneness of life, and the unnaturalness and injustice of all special favoritism. The colored woman feels that woman's cause is one and universal . . ." (Collins, 1991).

This womanist principle can guide the womanist anthropologist in seeking an anthropology that is both humanist and whole. As a womanist anthropologist, I believe that I must empower myself through knowledge of anthropological history and theory, knowledge of the political and historical contexts in which anthropology has developed, and knowledge of Black people's historical relationship to anthropological ideas, despite the apparent invisibility of people of the African diaspora in the founding of the discipline.

Obviously, knowledge of anthropology's historical and theoretical roots is critical to the development of a contemporary anthropological scholar. We must know the questions posed by our disciplinary predecessors, and we must have more than a passing familiarity with the written records of their observations and ideas. We also must know of the passion with which the early anthropologists pursued their interests, and the forces that allowed them to follow their curious and brilliant minds. However, does this knowledge provide a balanced historical perspective for all contemporary research interests? As anthropology evolves, can traditional theories provide cogent theoretical foundations for contemporary anthropological analyses?

The answers to both of these questions are "no" and "no." One of the ways in which I have sought to address the issue of humanness and wholeness in anthropology is through pedagogy. In the spring of 1993, I developed a course which focuses on African-American anthropology (Rodriguez, in press). Because "Field Studies" is offered through the Africana Studies Department, the students who enroll in the course are typically Black and Africana Studies majors as well. These undergraduates engage in action-oriented, ethnographic research in Black communities.

While the students are introduced to anthropological theory and methodology, they also explore the role of anthropology in race relations and the ways in which people of the African diaspora have participated in anthropology since the nineteenth century. Equipped with this historical awareness (which is rarely presented in anthropological teaching, particularly at the undergraduate level), the students consider some of the issues facing Black anthropologists who choose to study people of the African diaspora. Students also are challenged to consider some ways in which their research can provide some solutions to problems facing the communities they study.

Upon completion of the class, students typically are intrigued by anthropological inquiry and often consider double majors in Africana Studies and anthropology. As a result of their research experiences, several students have applied to graduate programs in anthropology. More importantly, the womanist vision of wholeness and humanness has contributed to a class in which students are able to generate or regenerate interest in communities from which they themselves may have come. Through this vision of wholeness and humanness, Black students may be more likely to consider their social and political responsibilities to their communities, rather than view education as a means of separating themselves from their communities.

Another womanist principle that contributes to the creation of a womanist voice in anthropology is not only self-determination but self-definition. Collins (1991) contends that having the power of self-definition is essential for Black women. This concept supports the understanding that the womanist scholar must shape an anthropology that speaks to her interests despite others' concerns about "objectivity" in studying subjects so similar to herself. The issue of the Black scholar's objectivity in studying people of the African diaspora is one with which early Black anthropologists grappled, and one which contemporary graduate students often discuss.

As an example of the historical nature of this issue, Drake (1980) maintains that the few Blacks who practiced anthropology in the 1950s were discouraged from conducting fieldwork in Africa. Black scholars received little support to study in Africa, because it was felt that their presence might offend the colonial powers who were highly visible on the continent during the imperialistic 1950s. Further, it also was felt that anthropological inquiry by Blacks in Africa would not be valid because Black scholars could not be objective about Africa (Drake, 1980). In this case, both politics and science teamed up to prevent the study of Blacks by Blacks.

With America's growing conservatism, and with the gradual but steady increase in Black conservatives who are rewarded with leadership positions, we as scientists once again may hear that our interest in people of color does not warrant fellowship or grant dollars. It is very clear that current political forces are attempting to define our scholarly and intellectual boundaries even more stridently than ever, and to dictate what does and does not constitute scientific inquiry.

Nevertheless, the womanist principle of self-definition informs womanist anthropologists that our intellectual interests in the lives of people of Africa and its diaspora are both scientifically legitimate and socially valuable. This womanist principle by no means dictates that Black and/or womanist scholars only must study women and men of Africa and its diaspora. Rather, the principle of self-definition in womanist thought encourages womanist scholars to study any aspect of any culture, with the knowledge that such research is legitimate and valid. Further, regardless of her scholarly interests, the self-defined womanist anthropologist must be aware of the politics of her interactions with any group she chooses to study.

Teaching activist community research and developing historical ethnographies on local Black women activists are two examples of anthropological work that is informed by a womanist epistemology. Both of these projects speak to the merging of theory and action, which is indeed one of the most important goals of a transformed anthropology.

3

Anthropology
Kinship and Gender

In 1987 Jane Fishburne Collier and Sylvia Junko Yanagisako described their goal as putting gender "at the theoretical core of anthropology" by "calling into question the boundary between the two fields" of gender and kinship. That kinship studies should have appeared as an autonomous field, distinct and perhaps even resistant to the analysis of gender, was attributed largely to the particular conception of society espoused by the structural-functionalists, led by A.R.Radcliffe-Brown.Like many feminist anthropologists, Collier and Yanagisako questioned the degree to which discussions of women's lives were relegated to considerations of the domestic sphere and to reproductive function. They repudiated assumptions (explicit or implicit) that the maternal-child relation is invariant across time and space, and they cast suspicion on the tendency to see historical change as a factor relevant only to political and economic systems in the public domain, while familial life was presumed to be constant and unchanging. Finally, they discerned in structural-functionalist writings an erroneous presumption that all societies have institutional functions that are comparable, even when the forms of theirs institutions differ.

Many of the questions articulated by Collier and Yanagisako generated productive new approaches to ethnography. In a companion essay in the same volume, they went on to pose another question which resurrected and refined one of Margaret Mead's (1901–1978) earlier challenges - namely, "What social and cultural processes cause men and women to appear different from each other?" In *Male and Female* (1949), Mead had observed that anatomical differences provide only the first point of identification for boys and girls, and noted that, from that moment on, children would compare themselves to others and in this fashion acquire a socially mediated sense of sexual selfhood based on traits and characteristics privileged or denigrated by their elders. Her own conception of sexual difference was indebted to Sigmund Freud's (1856–1939) analysis of sexuality in *Three Essays on the Theory of Sexuality* (1905) and retained his binary conception of sexual difference as based on biological antinomy. However, Mead disagreed with Freud's students and with his own postulation of a universally phallic stage in female development.

Against the backdrop of the Cold War and a burgeoning arms race, Mead's contribution to the ongoing tradition of gender studies is rooted in the denaturalizing comparativism that she embraced as the ground of critical anthropology: "If we recognize that we need every human gift and cannot afford to neglect any gift because of artificial barriers of sex or race or class or national origin, then one of the things we must know is where the assumed differences between the sexes are mere elaborations of unimportant differences that can be dealt with easily in this invention-conscious world". To this end Mead emphasized the extraordinary diversity of conceptions of ideal maleness and femaleness across cultures, and on this basis hypothesized the possibility that children might even disavow some of their "biological inheritance" in order to achieve a social ideal of masculinity or femininity. She thereby introduced a conception of maleness and femaleness as a social construction irreducible to the physiological basis in which it grounds itself.

Nonetheless, the question of gender remained secondary to that of kinship, where it constituted an assumption rather than object of inquiry for several more decades.

Kinship theory in anthropology can be traced to Lewis Henry Morgan's treatise, *Systems of Consanguinity and Affinity of the Human Family* (1870), a work that would considerably influence Friedrich Engels, as well as both structuralist and Marxist anthropologists. Morgan argued that the family as an institution emerged only after a period of promiscuity and then incestuous cohabitation, and that it depended on the creation of a law of exogamy. Nearly a century later, Claude Lévi-Strauss (b. 1908) revived and revised Morgan's argument when he claimed that the incest taboo constituted the archetypal form of all law, and that it marked the threshold between nature and culture. Although he asserted that sexuality was the origin of sociality, insofar as sexual desire is an instinct that requires another person, it was the incest taboo that transformed consanguinity into alliance by rendering women as "the supreme gift" in his analysis.

ANTHROPOLOGY - RITUALS OF BECOMING

One of the primary assumptions of contemporary gender theory is the social construction of gender, but although this core idea is closely linked to the recognition that kinship and even parentage is not a biological matter but a social one and that descent is a mode of recognizing children rather than transmitting genetic material, the connection between the theorization of gender and kinship was not immediately obvious to anthropologists of the early twentieth century. Even Bronislaw Malinowski, who claimed that sex must be understood as but one moment in a vast system comprising love, eroticism, mythology, courtship, kinship, family life, economic and religious practices, and tribal structure, devoted little time to a consideration of how boys and girls come to assume the qualities that make them socially recognizable as such. For him, sexual and social maturation were inimitably linked, but his attention was narrowly focused on the transformation of willful desire between two persons - expressed most purely and freely by adolescents - into a relation capable of self-negation in parenting. Malinowski's most profound insight may have come in his argument that kinship is not so much a matter of sexual intercourse as it is a sublation of dyadic relations into triadic ones, of interpersonal intimacies into intergenerational dependencies. Yet, because his concern lay with the functional appropriation of individual facts for social ends and because his concept of function was so immediate, Malinowski never seems to have considered the difficulty of achieving what Margaret Mead would later term ideal maleness or femaleness.

For the majority of early writers on kinship, gender was the axiomatically binary ground on which kinship and marital exchange could be erected. In Western theoretical traditions, this axiomatic quality of binary gender differences naturalizes itself in biological metaphors to such an extent that gender difference collapses into sexual difference and appears as anatomically and/or genetically determined. Two main sources of critique inform the development of the social constructivist analysis of gender per se. The first is the vast literature on ritual and corporeal practice, from the archive of which anthropologists have assembled their cases for the relativity of somaticization and sexualization. The second is to be found in the reconsideration of earlier theoretical arguments about such practice, especially as developed in the 1970s and 1980s under the influence and in the context of new social movements, especially feminism. This discussion begins with the consequences and potentialities of ritual theory for gender analysis.

In 1909 Arnold van Gennep undertook to formalize a theory of the rites associated with transitional stages of life and offered a tripartite model consisting of separation, liminality, and re-aggregation to explain their operations. Later elaborated by Victor Turner (1969) in a manner that highlighted the ambiguity and potential subversiveness of the interstitial phase, the notion of the ritual production of social status entailed a recognition that the bodily identity of a person is an inadequate determinant of her or his social identity. Indeed, Van Gennep made the brilliant observation that initiation rites work by overcoming the enormous chasm between biological puberty and what he termed "social puberty." Even more radically, he suggested that these rites do not so much mark puberty as they produce sexuality, removing people from an asexual state and birthing them as either male or female sexual subjects, who can then enter into legitimate sexual and especially reproductive relations with other adults. Van Gennep's radicalism has been mainly forgotten, but feminist anthropology has reclaimed his constructivist insight following a rapprochement with linguistic theory and dialectical materialism, the invention of "gender" as a category, and the emergence of a political project that has made the pursuit of resistance and other forms of counter-hegemonic practice the goal of much comparativist work.

ANTHROPOLOGY - MATERIALISM AND DIALECTICAL ANALYSIS

Rubin began her essay by asserting that "there is no theory which accounts for the oppression of women ... with anything like the explanatory power of the Marxist theory of class oppression" . She concluded by calling for a new version of Engels's *The Origin of the Family.* Efforts to integrate gender analysis with class analysis and with more generally materialist concerns have taken a number of forms since Rubin's article was published. In general these have concerned the relationship between unremunerated housework and the reproduction of labor, the impact of colonialism and capitalist penetration on gender relations in local cultures, the new international division of labor, and the feminization of geopolitical regions.

Historically concerned with small-scale societies and under-girded by the assumption that the most elementary form of any social phenomenon reveals an essence that carries across other manifestations, Marxist anthropologists imagined the division of labor between men and women to be identical to the division between productive and reproductive functions. However, during the 1980s and beyond, questions of production and reproduction and of the status of women were increasingly reframed in terms of the colonial encompassment of indigenous economies and the new international distribution of labor. This led to studies of new logics of power, such as those by which class has displaced status as a rubric of social stratification in some places. It also generated analyses of new competitive relations between men and women as economic power became unified in a single (generalized) commodity form where previously it had been divided among regimes of value. In these contexts gender became the contested mechanism for regulating access to economic resources. A vast literature also developed in response to the emergence of transnational labor networks and the establishment of new manufacturing zones in the digitizing global economy of multinational finance. By attending to the gendered organization of value, and not merely the symbolic value (or lack thereof) accorded women (Weiner), it has become possible to speak of a "feminization of the global economy."

Materialist analyses of these latter processes, which take place in a transnational realm that exists both above and below the level of the nation-state, have perhaps inevitably privileged economic questions, but they have often stopped short of economic determinism. Dialectical analysis has been summoned here as a means of recognizing the degree to which indigenous forms of familial and social organization remain resilient or resistant in the face of encompassment by multinational capital, global finance, and other transnational forces. But a dialectical approach to the transformation of gender (or the sex/gender system) must actually redouble itself. For it not only entails the recognition that local life-worlds are transformed without being destroyed in the modern moment (hence it must examine the dialectics between the local, the global, and the emergence of transnationally comparable values like locality), it also requires a reading practice that seeks to comprehend, from two distinct locations or perspectives, the facts of these historical processes. Reading for resistance became a primary objective of much work in the field of gender studies during the last two decades of the twentieth century. Promising in many regards, it has nonetheless been weakened by a tendency to conflate the fact of social and structural specificity with an intentionalized and often strategic, or at least tactical, opposition to the forces of both foreignness and new inequity.

Resistance was the term by which gender studies sought to rescue itself from the absolutist pessimism of structuralist universalism as well as economic and cultural determinism. Under the influence of Clifford Geertz, American anthropological analysis of culture had tended to represent culture as a system of shared signs or symbols. Conceived as a theoretical refutation of the economic determinism that cruder forms of Marxism espoused, culturalism nonetheless reproduced its problematic negation of agency while also eviscerating any recognition of structural contradiction. Resistance conceived within the culturalist tradition thus came to be imagined as a possibility originating in the critical reading and interpretation of those signs and symbols that comprised cultural totalities. Ironically, the language of resistance permitted two distinct theoretical traditions to converge, those of the Italian Marxist Antonio Gramsci (1891–1937) and the French libertine philosopher Michel Foucault (1926–1984). It was a thematically and methodologically driven reading of Foucault's later writings on sexuality that informed the genealogical turn in gender studies and in anthropology more generally.

ANTHROPOLOGY - FOUCAULT AND THE GENEALOGY OF SEXUALITY

Although Foucault's early writings attempted to excavate the sedimented structures of thought in a particular moment (and the discontinuous relations between moments), it was his development of a retrospective historiographical mode that made his writings on sexuality appear exemplary for historicist anthropologies concerned with the emergence of particular sex/gender systems. The first volume of *The History of Sexuality,* in particular, was quickly hailed for its demonstration of what the genealogical method could offer gender studies - although many theorists mistook a mere reversal of chronology for Foucault's more radical demand that ontological thought be surrendered in favor of a negative concept of becoming.

Two main contributions were recognized. Firstly, Foucault argued that prohibition does not work to contain or repress that which it outlaws but rather cultivates its sanctioned objects in a new mode. The sexual repression of the Victorians, for example, did not so much eliminate an interest in sex as it permitted the extension of erotic pleasures into the domain of language, such that talking about sex - even in the form of denunciation - could be seen as one more incitement of sex, while making speech itself a scene of excitement. The second contribution lay in its analysis of the relationship between sexuality and political power in Western cultures.

At the end of *History of Sexuality,* Foucault described the emergence of a new political technology, one marked by power's investment in life, in the control and management of human beings as productive entities whose health and well-being it assiduously cultivated. Discourses on sexuality, and on so-called healthy sexuality, were coterminous for him with the displacement of centralized power by diffuse forms of discipline and control that saturated all dimensions of the life-world. Foucault described this new technology as one that entailed a "power over life" rather than a "right of death" and designated it as "biopower." From Europe's eighteenth century onward, biopower worked through the surveillance of sexual practice and by placing same-sex intimacies under increasingly violent prohibitions, as the demand for total productivity and intentionalized reproductivity intensified in the modern industrial era. In other contexts, he admitted, the organization of power over life might take other forms, and might structure subjectivity in terms other than those of sexuality, but his primary focus was the more familiar history of European modernity.

In Europe and elsewhere, Foucault's claim that homosexuality was a modern invention, the product of discourses upon normalcy and sexual health, scandalized many scholars and was initially misunderstood by many to imply the relatively recent appearance of same-sex intimacy. Foucault made no such claim; he was instead identifying a moment in which practice and identity were merged by virtue of new representational logics. This merging produced not same-sex intimacies but the figure, and henceforth, the felt experience, of the homosexual.

Although his exemplary case study came from the archives and entailed the story of an ambivalently sexed figure, Herculine Barbin, who was forced to assume a male identity by French medical and police authorities, feminists quickly observed that Foucault's analysis failed to distinguish between sexuality as it came to be configured for women and men. In other words, they argued that sexuality without consideration of gender could only reproduce the relative claim that the figure of maleness has on universality in Western philosophical discourse. Feminist writers were quick to observe, for example, that the prerogative of transvestism is often limited to members of one gender and suggested that the distribution of this prerogative might itself be indicative of power in the organization of local sex/gender systems. At the same time, however, many anthropologists, influenced by the burgeoning phenomenon of gay and lesbian studies, also saw in the tale of Barbin an exemplary ur-figure of modernity's sexualizing violence. A vast array of cross-cultural studies were devoted to excavating eras in other places where sex and gender was (or continues to be) organized according to less rigorously binary structures. And older reports of female husbands, institutionalized transvestism and androgyny, and legitimate same-sex intimacy were revisited with avidity.

The best of such work is assiduously historical, grounding itself in the meticulous scrutiny and translation of evidence from diverse archives and unofficial sources. However, much of the more ethnological comparativism has ignored Foucault's suggestion that biopower might be differently structured elsewhere and has sought analogues to European historical developments instead. As a result, it has borne a not inconsiderable resemblance to the oftentimes prurient studies of earlier sexology, especially when anthologized in collections devoted to the category of "third sex," "third gender," or comparative homosexualities. Historians, by contrast, have generated a series of supplementary histories that augment, clarify, or refute the suggestions made in Foucault's more programmatic moments, often bringing the same kind of analytic lens to the history of heterosexuality as he brought to homosexuality. And some anthropologists have attempted to understand the implications of Foucault's project for an analysis of institutional and discursive histories in the colonial context, paying particular attention to the organization of populations, institution of new educational systems, juridical rationalization, and forms of both public morality and sentiment that colonial regimes implemented.

Feminist critique of the masculinist bias in early Foucaultian analyses of sexuality has been followed by a bifurcation in the field and a proliferation of studies devoted to the analysis of masculinity and its relationship to systems of power, both within households and at the level of the state. These studies, whether overtly Foucaultian or not, consider the corporeal tactics and the ideological representations and values (such as machismo, honor, and valor) by which masculinity is cultivated in men, emphasizing the disjuncture between merely anatomical sex and social gender even when the two are conflated in local discourse (a 1998 study by Judith Halberstam extends this analysis in a consideration of what she terms "female masculinities"). The Foucaultian turn might thus be read as the process by which the feminist political slogan "the personal is the political" gets inverted, such that the political is understood as that which generates embodied persons. In any case, it generated a renewed theory of the importance of ritual in the constitution of sexual and gendered difference.

ANTHROPOLOGY - REPEATING RITUAL

Feminism and gay studies, Foucault and the study of ritual, came together in the work of Judith Butler. In an eclectic theoretical blending of Foucault's discourse analysis, J. L. Austin's *How to Do Things with Words* (1962) linguistic pragmatics, and Hegelian dialectics tempered by Louis Althusser's notion of interpolation, Butler demonstrated that the principle of reiteration (etymologically linked to rite and ritual) can be seen in the myriad gestures of daily life. Although her early work implied a degree of voluntarism not present in Austin's theory, Butler's later writings recognize that these gestures or "repeated acts" take place "within a highly rigid regulatory frame," and they produce, for Butler, gendered bodies not only as representations but as materialized and sensuously experienced entities. They do so in two senses. Repetition generates habitual forms that are recognized within the social world; and they subject persons to ideals but in a manner that leaves them relentlessly deficient. Transforming Althusser's notion of ideological hailing as that gesture by which power names and thereby summons a person in the terms that power confers, Butler suggests that all individuals are both hailed and made to bear the unconscious knowledge that they cannot, by definition, achieve the image that power gives to them as ideal. Compulsively enacting the forms that would demonstrate comformity to gender ideals, most train their bodies to become sexually legible. For some, however, a consciousness of the gap between ideal gender and materially actual difference can become the basis for resistance to the sex/gender system.

Butler's work reached anthropology in the wake of Pierre Bourdieu's "practice theory" and was often read as the politically radical version of the French sociologist's reinvigorated structuralism. Bourdieu had analyzed what he termed the "doxa" of everyday life and suggested that architectural forms shape and constrain bodily gesture, inculcating dispositions that then cause people to act in ways that exteriorize the social structure. His description of this process in Kabyle villages suggested a necessary complementarity between men's and women's acts as the instruments for realizing a whole world otherwise divided between public and private domains. Bourdieu's notion of practice gave new life to Marcel Mauss's original assertion in

1968 that no bodily act, not even sex, is natural, and that the ideational or symbolic order of a given culture is something that exists in the body. This corporeal unconscious is never fully amenable to objectification in language and is actually dissipated in the moment that it becomes articulate. Unlike Bourdieu's vision of practice, which seemed incapable of explaining change, however, Butler provided a theory of how unconscious bodily sensitivities could become the basis of conscious opposition to the predominating sex/gender system.

Whether in response to Bourdieu or to Butler, the result was a proliferation of works broadly construed as anthropologies of the body. Many of these attempted to examine corporeal practices that appeared to be conspicuously implicated in the unequal distribution of power and the material constraint of women's sexual and sensual capacities. Many were also driven by the ambition to discover the different ways in which women interpreted these practices, so as to discover in them unexpected freedoms or self-experiences that differed from, and perhaps contradicted, the ideological representations of dominant discourse. Here the anthropology of the body met a globalizing feminist consciousness and a new politics of representation.

ANTHROPOLOGY - POWER, REPRESENTATION AND RESISTANCE

Finding resistance in the interpretation of genital cutting - as, for example, freedom from desire, or in the experiences of factory workers possessed by spirits - as liberation from the monotonies of the assembly line may seem odd. Are these painful and debilitating experiences the ground of resistance? Or the symptoms of a system that makes women the handmaids of their own oppression? Can resistance be unconscious? And if so, is resistance a sign of agency?

In direct counterpoint to these readings of the subjectivityless women in whose bodies the social world demonstrated its own violence and limitations there emerged in the 1980s another body of literature whose aims were to give expression to the conscious agencies of dominated women and other minorities, especially in the Global South.

Giving voice, or facilitating the self-expression of others - often through narrative forms that included biography and autobiography, fiction, poetry, and tokens of other expressive culture - became the commonplace gestures of well-intentioned anthropologists. These self-consciously feminist writers introduced a salutary counterbalance to those older texts in which the words of women, never mind their thoughts and experiences, were obliterated in generalizing and ostensibly genderless statements about "the way things are." The felicitous result: the textured life-worlds of soap-opera-watching housewives in Egypt, of ambitious but marginalized poor women healers and middle-class merchants on the Indonesian periphery, of devout Pentecostals in South Africa and proudly political mothers in Argentina, all entered the canon of ethnography, irrevocably transforming it in a humanist direction.

Works in this oeuvre share a certain descriptive quality. They also share an ambition to translate, both literally and figuratively, the experiences of others. Ironically, perhaps, the instruments of that translation have been the concepts of gender - including men and women - and experience. For this new anthropology has made its claim on the basis of a presumptive capacity for readers to recognize, as the experience of women (or men), the representations provided by anthropologists.

In light of all the anthropological evidence that being female or male differs between cultural contexts, and after all the theoretical labor aimed at debunking the universalist presuppositions of structural functionalism and then structuralism, there remains in feminist anthropology an indissoluble commitment to the transcultural and transhistorical viability of woman as a category of infinite translatability. The same can be said of gender, which appears to be an empty category but which nonetheless works through the presumption that the social difference organized through reference to sexual difference is distinct from all other kinds of difference.

This presumption has been called into question by a number of minority writers from the Global South. They have insisted that there is no material referent for the abstract category of "woman," and that, to the contrary, those named as women are subjects whose lives are determined by complex webs of politico-economic and therefore discursive forces, whether these be ones of race, class, location, or other principles. The implications of these claims for comparative gender studies have been enormous and deeply sobering, insofar as they suggest that there are not comparable communities of women whose experiences can be described and then compared. If some anthropologists ceded this point by advocating the self-representation of indigenous women (or by reading indigenous expressive forms as inherently self-representational), they did so in the face of an even more radical critique. The most acute proponent of that critique, Gayatri Chakravorty Spivak, argues that "subaltern women" cannot simply be ascribed or asked to inhabit the same kind of subjectivity that defines the position of white males in the European metropole. They cannot make themselves heard, except through a self-translation that rends them from their original location of invisibility and transforms them, through an ironically "enabling violence," into the kinds of beings whose speech is heard and recognized but only to the degree that it resembles that of its listeners.

Spivak's intervention made translation a question not only of technique but one determining the very possibility of gender studies. To be sure, translation had always been a question for comparative gender studies in anthropology, but it was defined much more narrowly. Originally it was recognized mainly in the comparative lexicons that anthropologists produced to demonstrate the relativity of kin terms (in places where men and women use different pronouns and kin terms). Since then it has been addressed through a variety of idioms, with silence and indirection often standing for women's incapacity to achieve or command a language of universal legibility. Conversely, silence and indirection have been read as indices of intentional resistance to dominant modes of communication (Gal). In a particularly innovative study of domestic intimacy in Sumatra, James T. Siegel demonstrated in 1969 how mistranslation, of the kind that lets women comprehend their treatment of men as patronizing indulgence (and hence indicative of their power) while also permitting men to read the same gestures as ones of deference (and hence testimony to their relative importance), actually facilitates gendered inequity and an odd kind of stability in Atchenese households.

Siegel's writings offer an alternative theory of translation, one in which incommensurabilities in language and interpretation do not so much prohibit communication as they facilitate incompletely comprehended social relations, ones infused by power, which is dissimulated in the gaps between interlocutors.

This does not make mistranslation a scene of resistance, any more than the translation of a subaltern woman's experiences into the representation of subalternity (for Western women readers) makes her an equal collaborator in global feminism. In very different ways, then, Siegel's and Spivak's insistence that power dissimulates itself in language and in claims to translational adequacy reveals the need for reflection upon the situation of speaking and reading. This problem is not mitigated by a recognition that globalization has brought about an increasing traffic in the terms and discourses emanating from the Anglo-American and European West.

Lexicalization and the transportation of idioms and concepts from one location to another especially those concerning gender and sexuality, women's rights and human rights - do not guarantee that their meanings will be constant or comparable. Reflecting on the instability of the category "woman" across continents, languages, and power divides, and recognizing that anatomy does not obviate translational problems, contemporary writers have also reflected on the history and intensification of instabilities in the so-called biological being of women in the context of technological modernity.

ANTHROPOLOGY - REDUX: SEX, KINSHIP AND AGENCY IN THE MACHINE AGE

Three main strands of thought have dominated the anthropological study of gender and technological modernity. The first of these, already discussed, concerns the organization of labor and the destructive or liberating effects of the commodity form and capitalism (industrial and financial) on the status of women, the organization of families, and the international division of labor. The second concerns the category of modernity itself and what it means for local life-worlds transformed by imperialism, colonialism, and multinational capital. Finally, analyses of gender and modernity have led to an interrogation of the consequences of new technological developments on reproductive possibilities, forms of kinship, the relationship between the pharmaceutical state and individual rights, bodily identity, and the transnational economy of suffering and its amelioration. It is the latter strand of thought - that which directly addresses the material conditions of mechanically dominated societies - that in the mid-1980s returned gender studies to its origins in kinship and the study of primitive society.

Donna Haraway's 1985 essay "A Manifesto for Cyborgs" threw down the gauntlet in this domain with its assertion that the corporeal and therefore sexualized body is not the discrete and encapsulated entity on which the fantasies of autonomous selfhood (and their attendant discourses of possessive individualism) are erected. Rather, they are discursively organized and technologically extended - opened and reformed, as it were - by everything from drugs to plastic surgery, shoes to artificial joints. This recognition of the human body as a pliant material entity, the boundaries of which cannot be known in advance, resonated with anthropological accounts of ritual reform, such as those that marked gendered maturity or sexual transition through forms of scarification, genital cutting, and tattooing, among other practices.

These insights have been especially fruitful in the feminist study of Western scientific discourse, medical practice in the

United States, and of medical representations more generally. Scholars have drawn attention to the violences and objectification that medicalization can entail. They have also revealed how the female form has been made to both figure and legitimate an invasive medical science whose invasiveness exceeds any possible utility.

Other writers have examined the ways in which economic logics enter and determine the conceptualization of bodies. Illustrative here is Emily Martin's (1994) argument that the contemporary concepts of bodily immunity and social epidemiology on which much AIDS research and prevention strategies have been based tends to valorize flexibility in a manner that mirrors contemporaneous economic logics. Bodies, in this sense, reproduce what the economy produces, but at the level of representation. By contrast, Linda Singer (1993) argues that while an intimacy is to be discerned between economy and sexuality in the age of epidemic (mainly but not exclusively the age of AIDS), it lies in the logic of the panic. Such panic, when linked to sexuality, would permit the increased regulation of persons and populations, and it would do so in the very moment that sexuality would be valorized and, indeed, valued in the terms provided by late capitalism. Singer's early insistence that AIDS be conceived as a biopolitical economy and not merely as a disease was paradigmatic for other scholars who, in very different ways, attempted to map the geopolitics of life, illness, death, and healing, in examinations of the pharmaceutical state and the transnational traffic in gendered bodies, prostheses, and drugs.

In the 1990s there also emerged a less dystopic approach to the question of gender and technological modernity, one that manifests a distinctly American conception of private, rights-bearing subjects whose sense of personal agency and entitlement permits them to instrumentalize, if not fully control, the discourses and technologies afforded by contemporary science, especially medical science. Rayna Rapp's 1999 account of amniocentesis, and many of the essays in Faye Ginsburg and Rapp's 1995 collection on reproductive technologies, certainly evince the tendency of women's reproductive functions to be appropriated through new technologies, and they reveal the degree to which a vast medico-technological and pharmaceutical apparatus is brought to bear on women in the interest of securing their reproductive functions (often reducing women to such functions). At the same time, however, their accounts of women who are forced into difficult choices by knowledge about fetal health or viability is supplemented by the sense that these "choices" can also become the ground of new agencies.

A concern with choice is also evident in gay, lesbian, and queer studies, where the problem of kinship continues to provide an orienting point for theoretical explorations of identity formation and social status. In many cases, such as Kath Weston's 1991 study of gay and lesbian families, entitled *Families We Choose,* sexual alterity becomes the iconic representation of absolute agency and self-determining choice. Although some thinkers have repudiated this model and proposed a genetic basis for homosexuality, anthropological evidence contradicts such efforts, and suggests that the category of homosexuality is not fully translatable across cultures. Same-sex intimacy is variously accommodated in a range of sex/gender systems without ever cohering into a single identity structure. Here again translation emerges as a crucial issue for comparative sexuality studies.

Gay, lesbian, and queer transnational alliances that, like those of earlier humanist feminisms, have arisen in the interest of producing, recognizing, and securing rights for individuals engaged in same-sex intimacy around the world. Violent repudiations of "homosexuality" and the designation of it as a Western perversion have been associated with new assertions of cultural sovereignty throughout the world, although, as in parts of Western Europe and the Americas, such disavowals symptomatize modernity as much as they resist a globalization of sexual cultures. Just as Western labors to solicit gender solidarity were forced to confront the competing demands for sovereignty made by individuals and collectivities (in the name of sexual and individual rights or gender asymmetry and cultural rights), so gay, lesbian, and queer activism faces a comparably agonistic confrontation between the notions of collaboration across difference and solidarity based in identification. The terrain of this conflict is often the idea of family.

FEMINIST THEORIES AND ANTHROPOLOGY

The following chapter represents briefly three phases of feminist thought in anthropology, beginning with the 1960s. The 1990s as a fourth or current phase are represented by a more specific discussion of two publications. The genesis of feminist thought in anthropology has been discursively embedded in the wider field of academic feminism and anthropological theory formation. Feminist ethnographers in the 1960s and 1970s sought to correct a 'male bias' in the discipline and promoted the study of 'women'. In the 1980s the focus shifted towards studying 'gender' as the category 'woman' came under critical scrutiny for its Euro-American and white bias. The shift to gender as an analytical category reflected that the concern with female lives could not just be about 'women' but about relations, practices and politics in which gendered identities were construed, and socially and culturally mediated. The multiple and contextual meanings of gender in relation to 'women' and 'men' dominated a feminist focus in the 80s and early 90s. Currently, this field of research is informed by a particular interest in epistemology and a search for anti-hierarchical and anti-exclusivist theorizing. This has been of particular interest for feminist ethnographers and their conceptualisations of 'fieldwork', the main site of anthropological knowledge formation.

CRITICAL ANTHROPOLOGY, PHILOSOPHY, AND ACADEMIC FEMINISM

Unlike philosophy, anthropology has the "intercultural" as its homeground. The very object of the discipline is laid out in the programmatic field of intercultural understanding, cross-cultural translation and mediation, and in the exploration of cultural difference. In gaining their intercultural knowledge anthropologists, unlike philosophers, do not emphasize reasoning, but rely greatly on observation and experience.

As critical philosophers discover the eurocentrism of their own discipline and the cultural bias of the term "philosophy" they also acknowledge that their intellectual undertakings have neither been neutral nor objective; instead, traditional philosophy's claim to universal knowledge rendered invisible the specific historical, political and social conditions on which it was based.

Intercultural philosophy seems to be dedicated to this self-reflexive stance and concomitant resolve to disrupt long-standing truths of the discipline. The programmatic aim outlined above notwithstanding, anthropology shares this concern. Despite an established practice of self-reflexivity, critical anthropologists have not ceased being haunted by the colonial bias of their discipline, which was, after all a historical by-product of colonial rule and expansion.

Academic feminism meets up with both, critical anthropology and critical philosophy at this point, as white Western feminists began to realize the ethnocentrism of their theories in the 1970s and 1980s and increasingly engaged in conceptualizing cultural difference.

In this review chapter the concern with "culture" is explored, as it emerged in the dialogue between feminism and anthropology. Hereby the focus is not on the concept of culture – but rather on issues of enculturated knowledge; something anthropologists set out to explore in others and something that makes their own explorations possible (and biased) at the same time.

THE FIRST PHASE: STUDYING WOMEN

Academic feminism as an interdisciplinary project, has its roots in a political reality that challenges confinement to one particular discipline. As a result, concepts and paradigms which developed from the 1960s onwards were shared as feminist philosophers, historians, literary therorists, anthropologists, sociologists, cultural theorists and others, engaged in a project that had a common political background – to take action against women's subordination.

The genesis of feminist thought in anthropology has been discursively embedded in the wider field of academic feminism and in anthropological theory formation. In the 1960s and 1970s feminists set out to correct the "male bias" in anthropology by focusing on women in the societies they studied. Anthropology, so the argument went, had been dominated by men as researchers and by male stereotypes about the position of women and therefore was replete with androcentric frameworks for the analysis of culture. The volumes edited by Reiter (1975) and Rosaldo / Lamphere (1974) set the agenda for feminist anthropology at the time. The studies were concerned with the societal organization of motherhood, with domestic work, marriage and sexuality, and many aimed at metacultural models that explained patriarchy as a universal structure.

Simone de Beauvoir

Many of these models were shaped by Beauvoirian (and structuralist) notions of the subject in human thought. It proposed that the subject is only in relation to an object which reflects the subject's negative image and guarantees its sovereignty. In Simone de Beauvoir's critique of the "Second Sex" which was based on traditional philosophies of the subject, woman is man's "other". Her "otherness" is understood not only as "being different from man" but as being so in a hierarchical sense of devaluation and exclusion.

In feminist theories and in a number of feminist ethnographies this model of oppositional otherness was equated with other binarisms and seen as universally existent in human thought and social organization: female was to male as nature to culture, domestic to public, body to mind, polluted to pure, passive to active and so forth. Feminist thinkers outside anthropology analyzed the dualist frames in European, particularly Cartesian thought, and its impact on modern notions of the "subject". These explorations revealed that the claim to universal subjecthood, based on reason and scientific rationalism was in fact grounded in male, white and western subjectivities.

During the initial period of making women visible in the academic field, feminists drew on the burgeoning cross-cultural research into "women's roles" undertaken by female anthropologists. Many of them contributed to the paramount image of the "universal woman" who shares sisterhood with others through shared oppression. The notion that it needs a woman to study women was also quite popular and advanced in so called "standpoint theories" of the 1970s and early 1980s. In anthropology this concept has never lost its value, as many societies do not allow unfamiliar men to interact with their women.

THE SECOND PHASE: DECONSTRUCTING THE UNIVERSAL WOMAN

Mary C. Lugones

In the 80s the claim to universalism changed. Feminist anthropologists studied "gender", the culturally variable understandings of what it means to be a woman or, with less emphasis, a man. Moore (1988) gives a thorough account of the shift from studying "women" to studying "gender" in the 1980's and to the rising controversial debates surrounding cross-cultural comparability. The shift to gender as an analytical category reflected the fact that the concern with female lives could not just be about "women" but about relations, practices and politics in which gendered identities were construed, and socially and culturally mediated.

This shift was, as Moore claims, partly due to the empirical evidence that understandings of gender were culturally specific and varying and partly to the strong criticisms black feminists directed against a white middle class bias in academic feminism in general. Moraga and Anzaldua 1981; Lugones and Spelman 1983; Lorde 1984; Hooks 1984; and Mohanty et al. 1991, were particularly influential texts in this respect. From the background of these criticisms feminists realized the differences among women and the insufficiency of the concept of gender in accounting for the experience of subordination. Black women and women of colour claimed that their gendered positions were deeply implicated in the issue of "race".

THE THIRD PHASE: THE MULTIPLE MEANINGS OF GENDER

Andrea Cornwall / Nancy Lindisfarne

An example for the diversion from pre-conceived ideas about male/female relations to the emphasis on contextual and culturally specific workings of "gender" was the volume edited by Sanday and Goodenoungh (1990), poignantly called Beyond the Second Sex. The ethnographic studies presented, relate to different cultural contexts (e.g. Africa, New Guinea, Sumatra, Middle East, USA) and do not adopt a uniform theoretical perspective. However, the essays collaboratively subscribe to the view that gender cannot be categorized in universal terms. They draw on womens' agency and resistance, on differences between women, and on the contextuality in which gender identities are crafted rather than assumed as fixed "roles". Gender emerges in its conflicting and ambivalent meanings within societies (not only "between" societies) and is de-emphasized as a sole determinant of oppression in human relationships.

These issues were pursued in the following years as gender increasingly came to be seen as implied in more complex processes of identity. Feminists worked on the assumption that subject formations are effected by a number of inequalities which complexly intersect. In the 90s feminist thought has fully embraced the notion of differences as an explanatory concept for identity and subordination. In other words, within three decades the question has shifted from, "why are all women oppressed?" (implying various binarisms) to "how is a female embodied subject constituted?" (implying all sorts of differences amongst which gender is just one). Or to put it in yet other terms, the transformation shifted from a Beauvoirian concept of "otherness" exclusively applied to women (in her view men do not have "gender", they are the universally human too) to a processual category that emphasized becoming much more than being. The transformation thus developed from "gender" to "gendering". "Gendering" found strong use value in anthropological thought, as it emphasized practice and cultural specifics, that is to say: localized, historicized human interaction and the everyday, culturally specific crafting of social (and sexual) identities. "Gendering" de-emphasized ready made assumptions about "man" and "woman" (e.g. Cornwall / Lindisfarne 1994).

At the same time, the insight into the "situatedness" of all knowledge had developed into a feminist concern with epistemology; feminists both inside and outside anthropology searched for alternative epistemologies which attempted to account for the identity of the thinker (her political, sexual, ethnic, economic, historical location) and for the position and partiality of the thought. In a self-reflexive embrace of epistemological "situatedness", that intrinsically shapes what 'we learn how to see' (Haraway 1991, 190) anti-hierarchical, anti-exclusivist theorizing should be realized (e.g. Visweswaran 1996).

'1990S' APPROACHES: INTERCULTURAL FEMINISMS

In what follows address two '90s' approaches: one that includes concerns with cultural difference in the broader framework of feminist thought, and another which is more rooted in anthropology and writes a feminist agenda into a particular ethnographic encounter. Here I am particularly concerned with the "intercultural" in feminism and the feminist in anthropology.

Susan Stanford Friedman's book Mappings (1998) is based on the authors scholarly field of literary studies in the United States. In intercultural, and "geopolitical" thinking and theorizing, she proposes to lead feminist theory "beyond" its current conceptualizations of gender and difference. These concepts have been vital in postmodern formations of feminist theory but nevertheless led to deadlock, since the pluralist discourse actually fostered separatism between different women and ultimately endangered feminism as a political project. This has to do with the fact that the gradual steps from the concept of "women" to "gender" and "beyond" was a theoretical journey from seemingly self-evident categories for people (i.e. "women") towards theories of subjectivity and identity, which necessarily had a pluralizing effect (i.e. old, young, rich, poor, black, white, lesbian, straight etc.).

Friedman cogently illuminates this development by differentiating six discourses on identity which evolved over the last three decades, commencing with the notion that "male oppression" was a principal index of female identity in mainstream Western feminism of the 1960s. Black women, particularly in the US, took issue with this notion and framed the discourse of "multiple oppression"; this was to remain powerful in as much as hierarchies of race, class, religion, ethnicity, or sexuality came to be understood as defining identity on the same par with gender.

In further approaches identity was then conceived of as a site of "subject positions" which are not necessarily all positions of subordination although nevertheless implicated in different axes of power. These positions are informed by class, race, gender, religion, sexuality, "and so forth", and function in 'multiple', 'contradictory', 'relational', 'situational' and finally, 'hybrid' ways in the formation of a person's subjectivity.

Incorporating the discourse of multiple identities into the analysis of culture (in Friedman's illumination of literary narrative) challenges three common assumptions: the privilege of gender 'as a determinant of identity' ; the isolated focus on women as objects of study; and the notion of a unidirectional flow of power (i.e. from men to women).

It also contests a separatist concept of "race" or, one may add, that of "culture", as is prevalent not only in feminist discourse but also in popular thinking on race in the United States with its emphasis on the white/black binary. Friedman stresses the need to develop more 'relational scripts' which take account of intercultural exchange, of power structures that operate not only across ethnic lines but also within ethnic groups, and of the commonalties and connections persons of different origins might have.

In elaborating on the need for moving on from the "difference discourse" Friedman then proceeds to the field of cultural identity and draws on recent anthropological theories on globalization. She focuses on the multiculturalist condition of Western societies and on a vision of breaking down the barriers between "White and Other". Friedman increasingly adopts spatial metaphors whilst writing on intercultural negotiations of identity – whose theorization itself transpires into 'migrancy', or 'criss-crossing all kinds of borders' .

These highly jargonized statements become more comprehensible when place is introduced as a "geopolitical axis", as actual locations in which people dwell or move and which play important roles in the formation of their identities. Every location on the globe is interlocked with wider regional, national and international politics, culture and economics. This makes identities far less locally fixed and determined as they are often imagined.

She presents us with some interesting answers. The often feminized and seemingly stable space of the Victorian home in Woolf's novels, for instance, turns out to embody 'geopolitical' connections such as, the Crimean War, British colonial rule in India, French food, or the British exploitation of the colonies that guarantees an upper class woman's economic freedom. These connections overtly or covertly emerge in Woolf's novels and mark the identity of the Victorian "home" as well as the subject position of the writer.

In a second step Friedman "geopolitically" compares Woolf's A Room of One's Own with Zora Neale Hurston's Their Eyes Were Watching God. Both writers explored in their respective novels a woman's search for "public" creative space in her particular cultural background. Whereas Hurston, the African American anthropologist and novelist, realizes that space on the porch, a place inscribed with male dominance, Woolf seeks a solitary room, equally symbolic of male prerogative .

In this "transatlantic" comparison Friedman suggests that both authors and their literary figures are located in a different cultural context but share a similar desire. She claims that only the comparative reading of both offers insights into local specificities as well as into translocal commonalties.

Susan Stanford Friedman

From an anthropological perspective such a "geopolitical" comparison is nothing new. It would have to include more specific explorations on what gender, desire, creativity, or the public means locally; or equally comparatively, if 'race' or 'racial politics' shapes Hurston's "porch", how does it shape Woolf's "room", or rather why is it absent from the "room"? In my view, the understanding that "race" equally shapes white identities (if only as a privilege), would be an important object of such a "geopolitical" study.

Evidently, Friedman's meandering through different literary texts, and her "travelling" in 'intertextual space across national boundaries' ends up in very particular representations of what a place is.

An anthropologists's physical travel across national boundaries, or a tourist's, or indeed a migrant's or a refugee's travel would surely reach different conclusions. Whereas "hybridity" is an interpretative framework for space chosen by Friedman with enthusiasm, some anthropologists may caution against the playfulness it suggests; some migrants may even be more concerned with fixing and homogenizing their place rather than with destabilizing it. For indigenous peoples on the other hand, fragmentation and "hybridity" of culture and place may be nothing new and promising. Rather, the scenario of "hybridity" may be representative of a painful aftermath of colonialism in their lives (Smith 1999).

FIELDWORK AS KNOWLEDGE PRODUCTION IN ANTHROPOLOGY

'While the West might be experiencing fragmentation, the process of fragmentation known under its older guise as colonialization is well known to indigenous peoples.

Fragmentation is not an indigenous project, it is something we are recovering from.'

Lind Tuhawi Smith

As stated above, in anthropology ethnographic fieldwork stands at the centre of knowledge production. This is the heart of the discipline but also the heart of problem, as the relationship between observer and observed is inscribed with colonialism and colonialist critique. As Linda Tuhiwai Smith, a Maori woman academic comments: 'The ethnographic 'gaze' of anthropology has collected, classified and represented other cultures to the extent that anthropologists are often the academics popularly perceived by the indigenous world as the epitome of all that is bad with academics.' (1999, 67)

These types of criticism hampered the discipline's self-consciousness anew in the 1980s and 1990s. However, this occurred not so much through listening to indigenous peoples (who have probably felt the way Smith describes it for several hundred years) but through the impact changing theories of the subject, postmodernism and poststructuralism had within Western academia. In other words, issues to do with subjectivity, representation and power emerged as pressing in the social sciences and humanities at large.

Within anthropology, representation and the relationship between "self" and "other" were themes around which ethnographic writing and fieldwork epistemologies were rethought. In particular the author who represents the "other" in a self-concealing detached fashion and thereby adopts a seemingly "scientific" viewpoint, became an object of criticism. This created space for reconceptualizing the fieldwork process as a personal encounter and as an intersubjective practice of learning and knowing. Further, the conventional forms of narrative representation as such became the field of criticism, as descriptive and classificatory styles were seen to mute, or exoticize the "other".

Feminist anthropologists in particular participated in these critical appraisals. Most central has been a concern with a particular epistemological web: the knowledge a fieldworker "brings" to the field, the knowledge process she engages in with local people, and the knowledge she produces after returning from the field. In as much as this triad is about understanding it is also about the limits of understanding.

CRAFTING SELVES

An impressive example in which the feminist epistemological agenda of "situated knowledges" and the anthropological critiques of representation (and much of what Friedman concerns about "spatial" identity) are ethnographically explored is Dorinne Kondo's book on a Japanese workplace, Crafting Selves (1990). Her account is rooted in discourses of identity and selfhood. Her own "self" as a Japanese American woman becomes unsettled while she experiences, in close everyday interaction with her Japanese co-workers, friends and relatives, the cultural imprint of her American identity as challenging and alien. In the Japanese setting in which she works and lives, "selves" emerge as contextual and "crafted" in relation to others and also to significant sites of identity, such as school, company, family, and nation.

She continuously aims at exploring the complex and contradictory sites of identity, with power being restrictive as well as creative, but hardly ever unidimensional. As a result, Japanese identities are not reified as "Japanese" but as quintessentially human. Gender is treated as one such site of identity where work on the shop floor is gendered by women and men as they interact and strategize dominant and subordinate positions.

HEIDI ARMBRUSTER

As she came "to learn how to see" through experiencing a recast of her own identity, she made "identity" and the "self" the objects of her research. It was her way of understanding the strangeness of the intercultural encounter, and consequently of "making sense". Her style of writing echoes the multilayered, complex and dynamic crafting of the identities she describes: personal self-reflexive accounts intermix with theoretical evocations, thick ethnographic descriptions, and dialogues with people she knew.

Friedman and Kondo take on board the notion that "gender" is not the site but one site of social identity. They displace "gender" from the privileged place it enjoys in feminist thought – without suggesting that this means the end of feminism.

4

Famous Anthropologists

MARGARET MEAD

Margaret Mead was a distinguished anthropologist, an intellectual and a scientist. She is the author of numerous books on primitive societies and she also wrote about many contemporary issues. Some of the areas in which she was prominent were education, ecology, the women's movement, the bomb, and student uprisings.

Margaret Mead was a woman who blended knowledge and action. Time, in fact, named her "Mother of the World" in 1969. In the political realm she served as a diplomat, without a portfolio, to many presidents in the areas of ecology and nutrition. She also had a great deal of concern about the role of science and technology in world politics.

Her Work

Her first major work was "Coming of Age in Samoa." This became a best seller and brought Mead prominence for the first time. Following her first work was the second from her South Seas voyage. This was titled "Growing Up in New Guinea." "Sex and Temperament in Three Primitive Societies" completed the trilogy on these native cultures. These works were significant, but hardly represent all of what Mead has done.

She continued to write on topics which focused on women's roles, childrearing, and other issues which clarify gender roles in primitive cultures and aspects of American society. These works include "Male and Female," "Balinese Character: A Photo Analysis," "Cooperation and Competition Among Primitive Peoples," "Continuities in Cultural Evolution," and "New Life for Old." She remained an active writer all of her life and her bibliography from 1925-1975 runs more than 100 pages.

Photography was not as common in Mead's lifetime as it is now. However, she did a tremendous job of integrating her photography with her writing skills. In doing this she was able to study culture at a distance. This had never been done before in this manner and served to be an advantage during World War ll in helping to understand the environment of Germany and Japan.

Education and Organizations

Mead earned her Bachelors of Arts degree in Sociology at Barnard College in New York. She then went on to Columbia University for her Masters and Ph.D. Following that she earned many honorary degrees and was a member of the American Academy on Arts and Letters. She also taught at Columbia University, New York University, Emory University, Yale University, The New School for Social Research, University of Cincinnati, and The Menninger Clinic. In 1965, she founded the urban anthropology department at N.Y.U. and in 1968 she founded the anthropology department at Fordham University.

At one time Mead was the President of each of the following prestigious organizations:

- American Anthropological Association,
- Anthropological Film Institute,
- Scientists Institute for Public Information,
- Society for Applied Anthropology.

Mead was the first ever elected president by membership in 1974 for the American Association for Advancement of Science. Although Mead's studies took her to the far reaches of the earth she did keep her base in the United States. This was at the American Museum on Natural History in New York. Here she began in 1926 as an assistant curator. In 1942, she was advanced to associate curator and a full fledge curator in 1961. In 1969, she was awarded curator emeritus. Her time at the museum culminated with a display of her own work in 1971.

Her Life

Margaret Mead was born in Philadelphia on December 18, 1901. She was the oldest of four children and both of her parents were educators. Both of her grandfathers were dead before her birth and she didn't really like her maternal grandmother. She had great fondness for her paternal grandmother. Along with her mom, these two women were the most supportive and influential people in her life.

In 1918, she graduated high school and was accepted into DePauw University. This was her fathers alma mater and he very much wanted her to attend university there. After one year at DePauw, despite her father's wishes, she transferred to Barnard College (Columbia University's sister school). At her new college she met Ruth Benedict, who became a close friend and soon persuaded Mead to become an anthropologist.

All this while she was engaged to a theology student, Luther Cressman and they married in 1923. She continued her masters work under a graduate fellowship and dreamed of having a big family. She was told by her doctor, however, that she would never be able to have children.

At the age of 23 in 1925, Luther and Margaret vacationed in New England together. At the end of this trip, he traveled on to Europe and she to Pago Pago (an American owned Polynesian island). In 1926, she returned to write her first book.

On her trip to Europe, she met a young psychologist from New Zealand, Reo Fortune. She immediately divorced Luther and married Reo. They settled in New Guinea and began an expedition that occurred from 1928 to 1929. During these first two expeditions Mead studied childhood development of the Manus culture and adolescent behaviors in the Samoan culture.

From 1931 to 1933, they continued to travel and Mead continued to study in New Guinea. In 1933, they assembled their third camp in Kenakatem. Here Mead made her great discovery that "human nature is malleable". She had witnessed three specific cultures; Arapesh, Mundugumor and the Tchambuli. Each culture displayed different gender role qualities. In one culture both the women and men were cooperative, in the second they were both ruthless and aggressive, and in the Thambuli culture the women were dominant and the men more submissive.

Due to these findings, Mead was one of the first people to propose that masculine and feminine characteristics reflected cultural conditioning (or socialization) not fundamental biological differences. In 1935, Mead returned to divorce Fortune. She then met and married Gregory Bateson. From 1936 to 1939 Mead and Bateson traveled together to cover more studies in Indonesia. Despite what the doctor told Mead she had one child with Bateson in 1939. She writes about this experience in her book "Blackberry Winter".

Her Image

Mead's most important role was as an interpreter of world events and trends to the American people. Not everyone, though, looked on with respect. At one time, she was on the board of directors of the YMCA. Some of her peers on the same board found her work scandalous. They even went so far as to call her first book, "Coming of Age in Samoa," a "sexbook". The governor of Florida called her a "dirty old lady" for her views on decriminalizing marijuana. And the wife on the Attorney General called her a "spook". These views did little to effect her stride. In fact, she liked to shake people up a bit. At one time, she introduced some pretty radical proposals. One of which was to pay students to go to college, while an other was to have a "trial" of "student" type marriage.

No matter what people said about her, she shaped the American family. Being married and divorced three times, being a mother, and a grandmother added to her credibility. She also felt that she did well in her field because she was a woman and because she was "feminine". For this reason, she preferred not to be associated with the term "feminist". She was a liberated woman, though, who kept her maiden name after being married. Jean Houston, Director of Mind Research in New York, once said of Mead, "She has one of the most 'filled' minds of any person I've come into contact with, and uses more of her intellectual capacity than any one I've known."

She was not an aloof intellectual. Mead kept friends for life and was generous with her money (especially for anthropological grants). She donated lots of time and spent countless hours lecturing to worthy groups. Her life was not filled with material extravagance.

Finale

In 1978, Mead died of cancer. Two years after death, her name was added to the leading feminist of the century. John Wiley, her editor, said of her, "She wrote as she spoke, very fluently and very fast. Clarity and sanity were her goals."

ZORA NEALE HURSTON

Zora Neale Hurston, (b.Jan. 7, 1891?, Notasulga, Ala.-d.Jan. 28, 1960, Fort Pierce, Fla.), novelist, folklorist, and anthropologist, was much responsible for the Harlem Renaissance being the watershed event in black America as delineated through literature that it was. Despite that she would later fall into disrepute because of her rigid views about civil rights, her earthy lyrical writing which lionized southern black culture has influenced generations of black American literary figures.

The early life of Zora Neale Hurston has been shrouded in mystery. While the majority of biographical accounts list the year of her birth as 1901, just as many list 1903, and in recent years 1891. For many years her birthplace was said to have been Eatonville, Fla. (the setting of many of her writings), however, recent evidence has placed it as Notasulga, Ala. Zora was the fifth of eight children of John and Lucy Ann Potts Hurston. Her father was a Baptist preacher, tenant farmer, and carpenter. At age three her family moved to Eatonville, the first incorporated black community in America with a then population of 125, and of which her father would later become mayor. To Zora Eatonville would become a utopia, glorified in her stories as a place black Americans could live as they desire, independent of white society and all its ways. The death of her mother when she was thirteen was a devastating event for Zora as she was "passed around the family like a bad penny" by her father for the next several years.

Upon reaching adulthood Zora was working as a domestic, still leading an itinerant life, with little schooling. She was in Baltimore in 1917, when through the aid of her employer she entered in Morgan Academy (the high school division of Morgan College (now Morgan State University). Though twenty-six years old at enrollment, she listed her age as sixteen and 1901 as the date of her birth. With her graduation in 1918, she matriculated at Howard University in Washington, D.C. Here she was inspired by the professor of philosophy and authority on black culture Alain Locke and decided to pursue a literary career. In 1921, her first short story "John Redding Goes to Sea" that was set in Eatonville was published in the Howard literary magazine *The Stylus*. In the following years she contributed several more stories to various magazines. One of these "Spunk" was published in the black journal *Opportunity* and caught the attention of such poets as Langston Hughes and Countee Cullen, who were active in a nascent artistic movement called the Harlem Renaissance. Zora transferred to Barnard College, an affiliate of Columbia University, where she was offered a scholarship in anthropology (she would take her B.A. in 1928). And being in New York City she quickly became a recognized member of the movement.

The Harlem Renaissance was a period during which black artists broke with the traditional dialectal works and imitating white writers to explore black culture and express pride in their race. This was expressed in literature, music, art, in addition to other forms of artistic expression. Zora and her stories about Eatonville became a major force in shaping these ideals. Additionally, she combined her studies in anthropology with her literary output. Studying under the famed professor of anthropology Franz Boas, she undertook field research (1927-1932) in the south with a fellowship from the Association for the Study of Negro Life and History during which she collected folklore and interviewed a former slave. Her results were published in the article "Cudjo's Own Story of the Last African Slaves" in 1927, which forty-five years later was found to have been plagiarized from *Historic Sketches of the Old South* by Emma Langdon Roche (1914). In 1930, Zora and Langston Hughes collaborated on a play *Mule Bone: A Comedy of Negro Life*. However, they became embroiled in a dispute over who deserved credit and the play never saw production.

Through a Rosenwald Fellowship (1934) and a Guggenheim Fellowship (1935-1936) Zora engaged in her most fruitful anthropological field research which produced her finest literature. In 1934 her first novel *Jonah's Gourd Vine* was published. Set in the fictional Sanford (a thinly disguised Eatonville), it tells of Jonah, a black Baptist preacher who is abundant in emotion and has a weakness for women. The *New York Times* critic Margaret Wallace stated it was "the most vital and original novel about the American Negro that has yet been written by a member of the Negro race." In 1935 *Mules and Men* was published. An investigation of voodoo practices in black America in focused on Florida and New Orleans in excellently recorded the folkways and songs of the rural south along with its main topic-the detail of which Zora gained from her own participation. The critic Lewis Gannett of the New York Herald Tribune stated: "I can't remember anything better since Uncle Remus."

From 1936 to 1938, Zora studied in Jamaica and Haiti on a Guggenheim Fellowship. This laid the groundwork for *Tell My Horse* (1938), a travelogue and a study of Caribbean voodoo. The reviews were mixed: praising it as vivid, keen, and humorous and criticizing it as tedious, sensationalistic, and misrepresentative. Notwithstanding, Zora's second novel *Their Eyes Were Watching God* (1937), which took place in Eatonville and told the story of a quadroon named Janie and her three marriages was in general praised as beautiful, touching, and irresistible.

In 1939, Zora's second-to-last novel *Moses, Man of the Mountain* was published. A modern version of the biblical story with a black voodoo magician named Moses as the main character, it was credited as being realistic and poetic, but it drew criticism for, as cited by the critic Louis Untermeyer, being unfulfilling as a whole though the characters were painted convincingly. In the following years Zora's literary output was sporadic. Her autobiography *Dust Tracks on a Road* (1942) and was a commercial success. Although written vividly and wittily, it suffered from gross inaccuracies as Zora attempted to paint a picture of her life according to the fantasy world she idealized. Her final novel *Seraph on the Suwanee* (1948), was set in Florida in the early twentieth century and oddly enough was about a white family named Meserve. Generally the critics considered this book unconvincing, though Zora's writing ability was noted.

Throughout her literary career Zora garnered much criticism for her failure to address the subject of racism as meted out by the white American society in her portrayals of black society. Zora seemed to view the entire world from the perspective of Eatonville, a place that blacks could be sovereign from all of white society, even the segregation that enveloped it as a southern town. Many of her contemporaries felt she was not seeing the whole picture, and as the civil rights movement burgeoned in the years after World War II and the majority of black writers adopted this as a theme, Zora's literary appeal waned. Then her reputation was scathed in 1948 when she was arrested for molesting a ten-year-old retarded boy; the charges were later dropped.

Despite this scandal, it was much of Zora's own doing that tarnished her reputation. She wrote an article in 1950 attacking the right of blacks to vote in the south, charging that votes were being bought. Then she railed the desegregation ruling in *Brown vs. the Board of Education of Topeka, Ks.* in 1954, on the grounds that black children do not need to go to school with white children in order to learn; to this many civil right leaders took umbrage. Zora wrote for such right wing publications as *American Legion Magazine* and campaigned for the ultraconservative Senator Robert Taft of Ohio for the GOP presidential nomination in 1952. This only alienated black America more and more.

Poverty and obscurity marked Zora's last years, during which she worked mostly as a domestic-as she had started out. She worked on a book *The Life of Herod the Great*, but never completed it. Illness finally overcame her when she suffered a severe stroke in 1959, after which she was committed to the Saint Lucie County Welfare Home in Fort Pierce, Fla. It was here that Zora Neale Hurston died of hypertensive heart disease on Jan. 28, 1960.

For all the opprobrium that Zora Neale Hurston received later in her career, the brilliance of her literary works cannot be denied. Future black writers such as Ralph Ellison, Toni Morrison and Alice Walker were greatly influenced by her books, and ironically they have addressed the issue of prejudice in their books. And any aspect of black culture that remains preserved today and continues to enlighten us owes its status in one way or another to Zora Neale Hurston.

SCOPE OF ANTHROPOLOGY

Anthropology is the whole history of man as fired and pervaded by the idea of evolution. Man in evolution-that is the subject in its full reach. Anthropology studies man as he occurs at all known times. It studies him as he occurs in all known parts of the world. It studies him body and soul together-as a bodily organism, subject to conditions operating in time and space, which bodily organism is in intimate relation with a soul-life, also subject to those same conditions. Having an eye to such conditions from first to last, it seeks to plot out the general series of the changes, bodily and mental together, undergone by man in the course of his history. Its business is simply to describe. But, without exceeding the limits of its scope, it can and must proceed from the particular to the general; aiming at nothing less than a descriptive formula that shall sum up the whole series of changes in which the evolution of man consists.

Anthropology is the child of Darwin. Darwinism makes it possible. Reject the Darwinian point of view, and you must reject anthropology also. What, then, is Darwinism? Not a cut-and-dried doctrine. Not a dogma. Darwinism is a working hypothesis. You suppose something to be true, and work away to see whether, in the light of that supposed truth, certain facts fit together better than they do on any other supposition. What is the truth that Darwinism supposes? Simply that all the forms of life in the world are related together; and that the relations manifested in time and space between the different lives are sufficiently uniform to be described under a general formula, or law of evolution.

This means that man must, for certain purposes of science, toe the line with the rest of living things. And at first, naturally enough, man did not like it. He was too lordly. For a long time, therefore, he pretended to be fighting for the Bible, when he was really fighting for his own dignity. This was rather hard on the Bible, which has nothing to do with the Aristotelian theory of the fixity of species; though it might seem possible to read back something of the kind into the primitive creation-stories preserved in Genesis. Now-a-days, however, we have mostly got over the first shock to our family pride. We are all Darwinians in a passive kind of way. But we need to darwinize actively. In the sciences that have to do with plants, and with the rest of the animals besides man, naturalists have been so active in their darwinizing that the pre-Darwinian stuff is once for all laid by on the shelf. When man, however, engages on the subject of his noble self, the tendency still is to say: We accept Darwinism so long as it is not allowed to count, so long as we may go on believing the same old stuff in the same old way.

How do we anthropologists propose to combat this tendency? By working away at our subject, and persuading people to have a look at our results. Once people take up anthropology, they may be trusted not to drop it again. It is like learning to sleep with your window open. What could be more stupefying than to shut yourself up in a closet and swallow your own gas? But is it any less stupefying to shut yourself up within the last few thousand years of the history of your own corner of the world, and suck in the stale atmosphere of its own self-generated prejudices? Or, to vary the metaphor, anthropology is like travel. Every one starts by thinking that there is nothing so perfect as his own parish. But let a man go aboard ship to visit foreign parts, and, when he returns home, he will cause that parish to wake up.

With Darwin, then, we anthropologists say: Let any and every portion of human history be studied in the light of the whole history of mankind, and against the background of the history of living things in general. It is the Darwinian outlook that matters. None of Darwin's particular doctrines will necessarily endure the test of time and trial. Into the melting-pot must they go as often as any man of science deems it fitting. But Darwinism as the touch of nature that makes the whole world kin can hardly pass away. At any rate, anthropology stands or falls with the working hypothesis, derived from Darwinism, of a fundamental kinship and continuity amid change between all the forms of human life.

It remains to add that, hitherto, anthropology has devoted most of its attention to the peoples of rude-that is to say, of simple-culture, who are vulgarly known to us as "savages." The main reason for this is that nobody much minds so long as the darwinizing kind of history confines itself to outsiders. Only when it is applied to self and friends is it resented as an impertinence. But, although it has always up to now pursued the line of least resistance, anthropology does not abate one jot or tittle of its claim to be the whole science, in the sense of the whole history, of man. As regards the word, call it science, or history, or anthropology, or anything else-what does it matter? As regards the thing, however, there can be no compromise. We anthropologists are out to secure this: that there shall not be one kind of history for savages and another kind for ourselves, but the same kind of history, with the same evolutionary principle running right through it, for all men, civilized and savage, present and past.

Anthropology is science in the sense of specialized research that aims at truth for truth's sake. Knowing by parts is science, knowing the whole as a whole is philosophy. Each supports the other, and there is no profit in asking which of the two should come first. One is aware of the universe as the whole universe, however much one may be resolved to study its details one at a time. The scientific mood, however, is uppermost when one says: Here is a particular lot of things that seem to hang together in a particular way; let us try to get a general idea of what that way is. Anthropology, then, specializes on the particular group of human beings, which itself is part of the larger particular group of living beings. Inasmuch as it takes over the evolutionary principle from the science dealing with the larger group, namely biology, anthropology may be regarded as a branch of biology. Let it be added, however, that, of all the branches of biology, it is the one that is likely to bring us nearest to the true meaning of life; because the life of human beings must always be nearer to human students of life than, say, the life of plants.

But, you will perhaps object, anthropology was previously identified with history, and now it is identified with science, namely, with a branch of biology? Is history science? The answer is, Yes. I know that a great many people who call themselves historians say that it is not, apparently on the ground that, when it comes to writing history, truth for truth's sake is apt to bring out the wrong results. Well, the doctored sort of history is not science, nor anthropology, I am ready to admit. But now let us listen to another and a more serious objection to the claim of history to be science. Science, it will be said by many earnest men of science, aims at discovering laws that are clean out of time. History, on the other hand, aims at no more than the generalized description of one or another phase of a time-process.

To this it may be replied that physics, and physics only, answers to this altogether too narrow conception of science. The laws of matter in motion are, or seem to be, of the timeless or mathematical kind. Directly we pass on to biology, however, laws of this kind are not to be discovered, or at any rate are not discovered. Biology deals with life, or, if you like, with matter as living. Matter moves. Life evolves. We have entered a new dimension of existence. The laws of matter in motion are not abrogated, for the simple reason that in physics one makes abstraction of life, or in other words leaves its peculiar effects entirely out of account. But they are transcended. They are multiplied by 'x', an unknown quantity. This being so from the standpoint of pure physics, biology takes up the tale afresh, and devises means of its own for describing the particular ways in which things hang together in virtue of their being alive. And biology finds that it cannot conveniently abstract away the reference to time. It cannot treat living things as machines. What does it do, then? It takes the form of history. It states that certain things have changed in certain ways, and goes on to show, so far as it can, that the changes are on the whole in a certain direction. In short, it formulates tendencies, and these are its only laws. Some tendencies, of course, appear to be more enduring than others, and thus may be thought to approximate more closely to laws of the timeless kind. But 'x', the unknown quantity, the something or other that is not physical, runs through them all, however much or little they may seem to endure. For science, at any rate, which departmentalizes the world, and studies it bit by bit, there is no getting over the fact that living beings in general, and human beings in particular, are subject to an evolution which is simple matter of history.

What are the functions of philosophy as contrasted with science? Two. Firstly, it must be critical. It must police the city of the sciences, preventing them from interfering with each other's rights and free development. Co-operation by all means, as, for instance, between anthropology and biology. But no jumping other folks' claims and laying down the law for all; as, for instance, when physics would impose the kind of method applicable to machines on the sciences of evolving life. Secondly, philosophy must be synthetic. It must put all the ways of knowing together, and likewise put these in their entirety together with all the ways of feeling and acting; so that there may result a theory of reality and of the good life, in that organic interdependence of the two which our very effort to put things together presupposes as its object.

What, then, are to be the relations between anthropology and philosophy? On the one hand, the question whether anthropology can help philosophy need not concern us here. That is for the philosopher to determine. On the other hand, philosophy can help anthropology in two ways: in its critical capacity, by helping it to guard its own claim, and develop freely without interference from outsiders; and in its synthetic capacity, perhaps, by suggesting the rule that, of two types of explanation, for instance, the physical and the biological, he more abstract is likely to be farther away from the whole truth, whereas, contrariwise, the more you take in, the better your chance of really understanding.

Sometimes, indeed, it is hard to say where science ends and policy begins, as we saw in the case of those gentlemen who would doctor their history, because practically it pays to have a good conceit of ourselves, and believe that our side always wins its battles. Anthropology, however, would borrow something besides the evolutionary principle from biology, namely, its disinterestedness. It is not hard to be candid about bees and ants; unless, indeed, one is making a parable of them. But as anthropologists we must try, what is so much harder, to be candid about ourselves.

This does not mean that human history, once constructed according to truth-regarding principles, should and could not be used for the practical advantage of mankind. The anthropologist, however, is not, as such, concerned with the practical employment to which his discoveries are put. At most, he may, on the strength of a conviction that truth is mighty and will prevail for human good, invite practical men to study his facts and generalizations in the hope that, by knowing mankind better, they may come to appreciate and serve it better. For instance, the administrator, who rules over savages, is almost invariably quite well-meaning, but not seldom utterly ignorant of native customs and beliefs. So, in many cases, is the missionary, another type of person in authority, whose intentions are of the best, but whose methods too often leave much to be desired. No amount of zeal will suffice, apart from scientific insight into the conditions of the practical problem. And the education is to be got by paying for it. But governments and churches, with some honourable exceptions, are still wofully disinclined to provide their probationers with the necessary special training; though it is ignorance that always proves most costly in the long run. Policy, however, including bad policy, does not come within the official cognizance of the anthropologist. Yet it is legitimate for him to hope that, just as for many years already physiological science has indirectly subserved the art of medicine, so anthropological science may indirectly, though none the less effectively, subserve an art of political and religious healing in the days to come.

The third and last part of this chapter will show how, under modern conditions of science and education, anthropology is to realize its programme. Hitherto, the trouble with anthropologists has been to see the wood for the trees. Even whilst attending mainly to the peoples of rude culture, they have heaped together facts enough to bewilder both themselves and their readers. The time has come to do some sorting; or rather the sorting is doing itself. All manner of groups of special students, interested in some particular side of human history, come now-a-days to the anthropologist, asking leave to borrow from his stock of facts the kind that they happen to want. Thus he, as general storekeeper, is beginning to acquire, almost unconsciously, a sense of order corresponding to the demands that are made upon him. The goods that he will need to hand out in separate batches are being gradually arranged by him on separate shelves. Our best way, then, of proceeding with the present inquiry, is to take note of these shelves. In other words, we must consider one by one the special studies that claim to have a finger in the anthropological pie.

Or, to avoid the disheartening task of reviewing an array of bloodless"-ologies," let us put the question to ourselves thus: Be it supposed that a young man or woman who wants to take a course, of at least a year's length, in the elements of anthropology, joins some university which is thoroughly in touch with the scientific activities of the day. A university, as its very name implies, ought to be an all-embracing assemblage of higher studies, so adjusted to each other that, in combination, they provide beginners with a good general education; whilst, severally, they offer to more advanced students the opportunity of doing this or that kind of specific research. In such a well-organized university, then, how would our budding anthropologist proceed to form a preliminary acquaintance with the four corners of his subject? What departments must he attend in turn? Let us draw him up a curriculum, praying meanwhile that the multiplicity of the demands made upon him will not take away his breath altogether. Man is a many-sided being; so there is no help for it if anthropology also is many-sided.

Again, he must be taught something about race, or inherited breed, as it applies to man. A dose of practical anatomy-that is to say, some actual handling and measuring of the principal portions of the human frame in its leading varieties-will enable our beginner to appreciate the differences of outer form that distinguish, say, the British colonist in Australia from the native "black-fellow," or the whites from the negroes, and redskins, and yellow Asiatics in the United States. At this point, he may profitably embark on the details of the Darwinian hypothesis of the descent of man. Let him search amongst the manifold modern versions of the theory of human evolution for the one that comes nearest to explaining the degrees of physical likeness and unlikeness shown by men in general as compared with the animals, especially the man-like apes; and again, those shown by the men of divers ages and regions as compared with each other. Nor is it enough for him, when thus engaged, to take note simply of physical features-the shape of the skull, the colour of the skin, the tint and texture of the hair, and so on. There are likewise mental characters that seem to be bound up closely with the organism and to follow the breed. Such are the so-called instincts, the study of which should be helped out by excursions into the mind-history of animals, of children, and of the insane. Moreover, the measuring and testing ofmental functions, and, in particular, of the senses, is now-a- days carried on by means of all sorts of ingenious instruments; and some experience of their use will be all to the good, when problems of descent are being tackled.

Of the special studies concerned with man the next in order might seem to be that which deals with the various forms of human society; since, in a sense, social organization must depend directly on material circumstances. In another and perhaps a deeper sense, however, the prime condition of true sociality is something else, namely, the exclusively human gift of articulate speech. To what extent, then, must our novice pay attention to the history of language? Speculation about its far-off origins is now-a-days rather out of fashion. Moreover, language is no longer supposed to provide, by itself at any rate, and apart from other clues, a key to the endless riddles of racial descent. What is most needed, then, is rather some elementary instruction concerning the organic connection between language and thought, and concerning their joint development as viewed against the background of the general development of society. And, just as words and thoughts are essentially symbols, so there are also gesture-symbols and written symbols, whilst again another set of symbols is in use for counting. All these pre-requisites of human intercourse may be conveniently taken together.

Coming now to the analysis of the forms of society, the beginner must first of all face the problem: "What makes a people one?" Neither blood, nor territory, nor language, but only the fact of being more or less compactly organized in a political society, will be found to yield the unifying principle required. Once the primary constitution of the body politic has been made out, a limit is set up, inside of which a number of fairly definite forms of grouping offer themselves for examination; whilst outside of it various social relationships of a vaguer kind have also to be considered. Thus, amongst institutions of the internal kind, the family by itself presents a wide field of research; though in certain cases it is liable to be overshadowed by some other sort of organization, such as, notably, the clan. Under the same rubric fall the many forms of more or less voluntary association, economic, religious, and so forth. On the other hand, outside the circle of the body politic there are, at all known stages of society, mutual understandings that regulate war, trade, travel, the celebration of common rites, the interchange of ideas. Here, then, is an abundance of types of human association, to be first scrutinized separately, and afterwards considered in relation to each other.

Closely connected with the previous subject is the history of law. Every type of association, in a way, has its law, whereby its members are constrained to fulfil a certain set of obligations. Thus our student will pass on straight from the forms of society to the most essential of their functions. The fact that, amongst the less civilized peoples, the law is uncodified and merely customary, whilst the machinery for enforcing it is, though generally effective enough, yet often highly indefinite and occasional, makes the tracing of the growth of legal institutions from their rudiments no less vitally important, though it makes it none the easier. The history of authority is a strictly kindred topic. Legislating and judging on the one hand, and governing on the other, are different aspects of the same general function. In accordance, then, with the order already indicated, law and government as administered by the political society in the person of its representatives, chiefs, elders, war-lords, priest-kings, and so forth, must first be examined; then the jurisdiction and discipline of subordinate bodies, such as the family and the clan, or again the religious societies, trade guilds, and the rest; then, lastly, the international conventions, with the available means of ensuring their observance.

Again, the history of religion is an allied theme of far-reaching interest. For the understanding of the ruder forms of society it may even be said to furnish the master-key. At this stage, religion is the mainstay of law and government. The constraining force of custom makes itself felt largely through a magnifying haze of mystic sanctions; whilst, again, the position of a leader of society rests for the most part on the supernormal powers imputed to him. Religion and magic, then, must be carefully studied if we would understand how the various persons and bodies that exercise authority are assisted, or else hindered, in their efforts to maintain social discipline. Apart from this fundamental inquiry, there is another, no less important in its way, to which the study of religion and magic opens up a path. This is the problem how reflection manages as it were to double human experience, by setting up beside the outer world of sense an inner world of thought-relations. Now constructive imagination is the queen of those mental functions which meet in what we loosely term "thought"; and imagination is ever most active where, on the outer fringe of the mind's routine work, our inarticulate questionings radiate into the unknown. When the genius has his vision, almost invariably, among the ruder peoples, it is accepted by himself and his society as something supernormal and sacred, whether its fruit be an act leadership or an edict, a practical invention or a work of art, a story of the past or a prophecy, a cure or a devastating curse. Moreover, social tradition treasures the memory of these revelations, and, blending them with the contributions of humbler folk-for all of us dream our dreams-provides in myth and legend and tale, as well as in manifold other art-forms, a stimulus to the inspiration of future generations. For most purposes fine art, at any rate during its more rudimentary stages, may be studied in connection with religion.

So far as law and religion will not account for the varieties of social behaviour, the novice may most conveniently consider them under the head of morals. The forms of social intercourse, the fashions, the festivities, are imposed on us by our fellows from without, and none the less effectively because as a general rule we fall in with them as a matter of course. The difference between manners and morals of the higher order is due simply to the more pressing need, in the case of our most serious duties, of a reflective sanction, a "moral sense," to break us in to the common service. It is no easy task to keep legal and religious penalties or rewards out of the reckoning, when trying to frame an estimate of what the notions of right and wrong, prevalent in a given society, amount to in themselves; nevertheless, it is worth doing, and valuable collections of material exist to aid the work. The facts about education, which even amongst rude peoples is often carried on far into manhood, throw much light on this problem. So do the moralizings embodied the traditional lore of the folk - the proverbs, the beast-fables, the stories of heroes.

There remains the individual to be studied in himself. If the individual be ignored by social science, as would sometimes appear to be the case, so much the worse for social science, which, to a corresponding extent, falls short of being truly anthropological. Throughout the history of man, our beginner should be on the look-out for the signs, and the effects, of personal initiative. Freedom of choice, of course, is limited by what there is to choose from; so that the development of what may be termed social opportunity should be concurrently reviewed. Again, it is the aim of every moral system so to educate each man that his directive self may be as far as possible identified with his social self. Even suicide is not a man's own affair, according to the voice of society which speaks in the moral code. Nevertheless, lest the important truth be overlooked that social control implies a will that must meet the control half-way, it is well for the student of man to pay separate and special attention to the individual agent. The last word in anthropology is: Know thyself.

ANTIQUITY OF MAN

History, in the narrower sense of the word, depends on written records. As we follow back history to the point at which our written records grow hazy, and the immediate ancestors or predecessors of the peoples who appear in history are disclosed in legend that needs much eking out by the help of the spade, we pass into proto-history. At the back of that, again, beyond the point at which written records are of any avail at all, comes pre-history.

Putting all kinds of evidence together, then, we get a notion, doubtless rather meagre, but as far as it goes well-grounded, of a hunter of the ice-age, who was able to get the better of a woolly rhinoceros, could cook a lusty steak off him, had a sharp knife to carve it, and the teeth to chew it, and generally knew how, under the very chilly circumstances, both to make himself comfortable and to keep his race going.

There is one other class of evidence on which the pre-historian may with due caution draw, though the risks are certain and the profits uncertain. The ruder peoples of today are living a life that in its broad features cannot be wholly unlike the life of the men of long ago. Thus the pre-historian should study Spencer and Gillen on the natives of Central Australia, if only that he may take firm hold of the fact that people with skulls inclining towards the Neanderthal type, and using stone knives, may nevertheless have very active minds; in short, that a rich enough life in its way may leave behind it a poor rubbish-heap. When it comes, however, to the borrowing of details, to patch up the holes in the pre-historic record with modern rags and tatters makes better literature than science. After all, the Australians, or Tasmanians, or Bushmen, or Eskimo, of whom so much is beginning to be heard amongst pre-historians, are our contemporaries-that is to say, have just as long an ancestry as ourselves; and in the course of the last 100,000 years or so our stock has seen so many changes, that their stocks may possibly have seen a few also.

Yet, rather more than half a century ago, when the Abbe Boucher de Perthes found palaeoliths in the gravels of the Somme at Abbeville, and was the first to recognize them for what they are, there was no small scandal. Now-a-days, however, the world takes it as a matter of course that those lumpish, discoloured, and much-rolled stones, shaped something like a pear, which come from the high terraces deposited by the Ancient Thames, were once upon a time the weapons or tools of somebody who had plenty of muscle in his arm. Plenty of skill he had in his fingers, too; for to chip a flint-pebble along both faces, till it takes a more or less symmetrical and standard shape, is not so easy as it sounds. Hammer away yourself at such a pebble, and see what a mess you make of it. To go back for one moment to the subject of eoliths, we may fairly argue that experimental forms still ruder than the much-trimmed palaeoliths of the early river-drift must exist somewhere, whether Mr. Harrison's eoliths are to be classed amongst them or not. Indeed, the Tasmanians of modern days carved their simple tools so roughly, that any one ignorant of their history might easily mistake the greater number for common pieces of stone.

On the other hand, as we move on from the earlier to the later types of river-drift implements, we note how by degrees practice makes perfect. The forms grow ever more regular and refined, up to the point of time which has been chosen as the limit for the first of the three main stages into which the vast palaeolithic epoch has to be broken up. The man of the late St. Acheul period, as it is termed, was truly a great artist in his way. If you stare vacantly at his handiwork in a museum, you are likely to remain cold to its charm. But probe about in a gravel-bed till you have the good fortune to light on a masterpiece; tenderly smooth away with your fingers the dirt sticking to its surface, and bring to view the tapering or oval outline, the straight edge, the even and delicate chipping over both faces; then, wrapping it carefully in your handkerchief, take it home to wash, and feast till bedtime on the clean feel and shining mellow colour of what is hardly more an implement than a gem. They took a pride in their work, did the men of old; and, until you can learn to sympathize, you are no anthropologist.

During the succeeding main stage of the palaeolithic epoch there was a decided set-back in the culture, as judged by the quality of the workmanship in flint. Those were the days of the Mousterians who dined off woolly rhinoceros in Jersey. Their stone implements, worked only on one face, are poor things by comparison with those of late St. Acheul days, though for a time degenerated forms of the latter seem to have remained in use. What had happened? We can only guess. Probably something to do with the climate was at the bottom of this change for the worse. Thus M. Rutot believes that during the ice-age each big freeze was followed by an equally big flood, preceding each fresh return of milder weather. One of these floods, he thinks, must have drowned out the neat-fingered race of St. Acheul, and left the coast clear for the Mousterians with their coarser type of culture. Perhaps they were coarser in their physical type as well.

To the credit of the Mousterians, however, must be set down the fact that they are associated with the habit of living in caves, and perhaps may even have started it; though some implements of the drift type occur in Le Moustier itself, as well as in other caves, such as the famous Kent's Cavern near Torquay. Climate, once more, has very possibly to answer for having thus driven man underground. Anyway, whether because they must, or because they liked it, the Mousterians went on with their cave life during an immense space of time, making little progress; unless it were to learn gradually how to sharpen bones into implements. But caves and bones alike were to play a far more striking part in the days immediately to follow.

The icy torrents that hollowed it in the limestone have eaten away rounded alcoves along the sides. On the white surface of these, glazed over with a preserving film of stalactite, we at once notice the outlines of many hands. Most of them left hands, showing that the Aurignacians tended to be right-handed, like ourselves, and dusted on the paint, black manganese or red ochre, between the outspread fingers in just way that we, too, would find convenient. Curiously enough, this practice of stencilling hands upon the walls of caves is in vogue amongst the Australian natives; though unfortunately, they keep the reason, if there is any deeper one than mere amusement, strictly to themselves. Like the Australians, again, and other rude peoples, these Aurignacians would appear to have been given to lopping off an occasional finger-from some religious motive, we may guess - to judge from the mutilated look of a good many of the handprints.

The use of paint is here limited to this class of wall-decoration. But a sharp flint makes an excellent graving tool; and the Aurignacian hunter is bent on reproducing by this means the forms of those game-animals about which he doubtless dreams night and day. His efforts in this direction, however, rather remind us of those of our infant-schools. Look at this bison. His snout is drawn sideways, but the horns branch out right and left as if in a full-face view. Again, our friend scamps details such as the legs. Sheer want of skill, we may suspect, leads him to construct what is more like the symbol of something thought than the portrait of something seen. And so we wander farther and farther into the gloomy depths, adding ever new specimens to our pre-historic menagerie, including the rare find of a bird that looks uncommonly like the penguin. Mind, by the way, that you do not fall into that round hole in the floor. It is enormously deep; and more than forty cave-bears have left their skeletons at the bottom, amongst which your skeleton would be a little out of place.

The neolithic men of western Europe often, though not always, polished their stone; the palaeolithic folk did not. That is the distinguishing mark by which the world is pleased to go. It would be fatal to forget, however, that, with this trifling difference, go many others which testify more clearly to the contrast between the older and newer types of culture. Thus it has still to be proved that the palaeolithic races ever used pottery, or that they domesticated animals-for instance, the fat ponies which they were so fond of eating; or that they planted crops. All these things did the neolithic peoples sooner or later; so that it would not be strange if palaeolithic man withdrew in their favour, because he could not compete. Prehistory is at present almost silent concerning the manner of his passing. In a damp and draughty tunnel, however, called

Mas d'Azil, in the south of France, where the river Arize still bores its way through a mountain, some palaeolithic folk seem to have lingered on in a sad state of decay. The old sureness of touch in the matter of carving bone had left them. Again, their painting was confined to the adorning of certain pebbles with spots and lines, curious objects, that perhaps are not without analogy in Australia, whilst something like them crops up again in the north of Scotland in what seems to be the early iron-age. Had the rest of the palaeolithic men already followed the reindeer and other arctic animals towards the north-east? Or did the neolithic invasion, which came from the south, wipe out the lot? Or was there a commingling of stocks, and may some of us have a little dose of palaeolithic blood, as we certainly have a large dose of neolithic? To all these questions it can only be replied that we do not yet know.

No more do we know half as much as we should like about fifty things relating to the small, dark, long-headed neolithic folk, with a language that has possibly left traces in the modern Basque, who spread over the west till they reached Great Britain-it probably was an island by this time-and erected the well-known long barrows and other monuments of a megalithic (great-stone) type; though not the round barrows, which are the work of a subsequent round-headed race of the bronze-age. Every day, however, the spade is adding to our knowledge. Besides, most of the ruder peoples of the modern world were at the neolithic stage of culture at the time of their discovery by Europeans. Hence the weapons, the household utensils, the pottery, the pile-dwellings, and so on, can be compared closely; and we have a fresh instance of the way in which one branch of anthropology can aid another.

as well as

only s

inherited

and all

Contrast

the phil

you say,

or again

immense

factors

mental

neither th

any quant

into ca

RACE FA

Race o

human na

something

practice w

A machine

together

can resolv

out of its

once and

5

Race and Environment

Race, let it not be forgotten, presumably extends to mind as well as to body and is not merely skin-deep. Race, in the only sense that the word has for an anthropologist, means inherited breed, and nothing more or less-inherited breed, and all that it covers, whether bodily or mental features. Contrast the stoical Red Indian with the vivacious Negro; or the phlegmatic Dutchman with the passionate Italian. True, you say, but what about the influence of their various climates, or again of their different ideals of behaviour? Quite so. It is immensely difficult to separate the effects of the various factors. Yet surely the race-factor counts for something in the mental constitution. Any breeder of horses will tell you that neither the climate of Newmarket, nor careful training, nor any quantity of oats, nor anything else, will put racing mettle into cart-horse stock.

RACE FACTOR

Race or breed was a moment ago described as a factor in human nature. But to break up human nature into factors is something that we can do, or try to do, in thought only. In practice we can never succeed in doing anything of the kind. A machine such as a watch we can take to bits and then put together again. Even a chemical compound such as water we can resolve into oxygen and hydrogen and then reproduce out of its elements. But to dissect a living thing is to kill it once and for all. Life is something unique, with the unique property of being able to evolve. As life evolves, that is to say changes, by being handed on from certain forms to certain other forms, a partial rigidity marks the process together with a partial plasticity. There is a stiffening, so to speak, that keeps the life-force up to a point true to its old direction; though, short of that limit, it is free to take a new line of its own. Race, then, stands for the stiffening in the evolutionary process. Just up to what point it goes in any given case we probably can never quite tell. Yet, if we could think our way anywhere near to that point in regard to man not that we should eventually succeed in forging a fresh instrument for controlling the destinies of our species, an instrument perhaps more powerful than education itself-I mean, eugenics, the art of improving the human breed.

To see what race means when considered apart, let us first of all take your individual self, and ask how you would proceed to separate your inherited nature from the nature which you have acquired in the course of living your life. It is not easy. Suppose, however, that you had a twin brother born, if indeed that were possible, as like you as one pea is like another. An accident in childhood, however, has caused him to lose a leg. So he becomes a clerk, living a sedentary life in an office. You, on the other hand, with your two lusty legs to help you, become a postman, always on the run. Well, the two of you are now very different men in looks and habits. He is pale and you are brown. You play football and he sits at home reading. Nevertheless, any friend who knows you both intimately will discover fifty little things that bespeak in you the same underlying nature and bent. You are both, for instance, slightly colour-blind, and both inclined to fly into violent passions on occasion. That is your common inheritance peeping out-if, at least, your friend has really managed to make allowance for your common bringing-up, which might mainly account for the passionateness, though hardly for the colour-blindness.

The development of the individual that results from such cell-union is no mere mixture or addition, but a process of selective organization. To put it very absurdly, one does not find a pair of two-legged parents having a child with legs as big as the two sets of legs together, or with four legs, two of them of one shape and two of another. In other words, of the possibilities contributed by the father and mother, some are taken and some are left in the case of any one child. Further, different children will represent different selections from amongst the germinal elements. Mendelism, by the way, is especially concerned to find out the law according to which the different types of organization are distributed between the offspring. Each child, meanwhile, is a unique individual, a living whole with an organization of its very own. This means that its constituent elements form a system. They stand to each other in relations of mutual support. In short, life is possible because there is balance.

This general state of balance, however, is able to go along with a lot of special balancings that seem largely independent of each other. It is important to remember this when we come a little later on to consider the instincts. All sorts of lesser systems prevail within the larger system represented by the individual organism. It is just as if within the state with its central government there were a number of county councils, municipal corporations, and so on, each of them enjoying a certain measure of self-government on its own account. Thus we can see in a very general way how it is that so much variation is possible. The selective organization, which from amongst the germinal elements precipitates ever so many and different forms of fresh life, is so loose and elastic that a working arrangement between the parts can be reached in all sorts of directions. The lesser systems are so far self-governing that they can be trusted to get along in almost any combination; though of course some combinations are naturally stronger and more stable than the rest, and hence tend to outlast them, or, as the phrase goes, to be preserved by natural selection.

It is time to take account of the principle of natural selection. We have done with the subject of variation. Whether use and disuse have helped to shape the fresh forms of life, or whether these are purely spontaneous combinations that have come into being on what we are pleased to call their own account, at any rate let us take them as given. What happens now? At this point begins the work of natural selection. Darwin's great achievement was to formulate this law; though it is only fair to add that it was discovered by A.R. Wallace at the same moment. Both of them get the first hint of it from Malthus. This English clergyman, writing about half a century earlier, had shown that the growth of population is apt very considerably to outstrip the development of food-supply; whereupon natural checks such as famine or war must, he argued, ruthlessly intervene so as to redress the balance. Applying these considerations to the plant and animal kingdoms at large, Darwin and Wallace perceived that, of the multitudinous forms of life thrust out upon the world to get a livelihood as best they could, a vast quantity must be weeded out.

Moreover, since they vary exceedingly in their type of organization, it seemed reasonable to suppose that, of the competitors, those who were innately fitted to make the best of the ever-changing circumstances would outlive the rest. An appeal to the facts fully bore out this hypothesis. It must not, indeed, be thought that all the weeding out which goes on favours the fittest. Accidents will always happen. On the whole, however, the type that is most at home under the surrounding conditions, it may be because it is more complex, or it may be because it is of simpler organization, survives the rest.

Now to survive is to survive to breed. If you live to eighty, and have no children, you do not survive in the biological sense; whereas your neighbour who died at forty may survive in a numerous progeny. Natural selection is always in the last resort between individuals; because individuals are alone competent to breed. At the same time, the reason for the individual's survival may lie very largely outside him. Amongst the bees, for instance, a non-working type of insect survives to breed because the sterile workers do their duty by the hive. So, too, that other social animal, man, carries on the race by means of some whom others die childless in order to preserve. Nevertheless, breeding being a strictly individual and personal affair, there is always a risk lest a society, through spending its best too freely, end by recruiting its numbers from those in whom the engrained capacity to render social service is weakly developed. To rear a goodly family must always be the first duty of unselfish people; for otherwise the spirit of unselfishness can hardly be kept alive the world.

Enough about heredity as a condition of evolution. We return, with a better chance of distinguishing them, to the consideration of the special effects that it brings about. It was said just now that heredity is the stiffening in human nature, a stiffening bound up with a more or less considerable offset of plasticity. Now clearly it is in some sense true that the child's whole nature, its modicum of plasticity included, is handed on from its parents. Our business in this chapter, however, is on the whole to put out of our thoughts this plastic side of the inherited life-force. The more or less rigid, definite, systematized characters-these form the hereditary factor, the race. Now none of these are ever quite fixed. A certain measure of plasticity has to be counted in as part of their very nature. Even in the bee, with its highly definite instincts, there is a certain flexibility bound up with each of these; so that, for instance, the inborn faculty of building up the comb regularly is modified if the hive happens to be of an awkward shape. Yet, as compared with what remains over, the characters that we are able to distinguish as racial must show fixity. Unfortunately, habits show fixity too. Yet habits belong to the plastic side of our nature; for, in forming a habit, we are plastic at the start, though hardly so once we have let ourselves go. Habits, then, must be discounted in our search for the hereditary bias in our lives. It is no use trying to disguise the difficulties attending an inquiry into race.

Racial features

If the plain man were to ask himself how, in walking down a London street, he distinguished one racial type from another, he would find that he chiefly went by colour. In a general way he knows how to make allowance for sunburn and get down to the native complexion underneath. But, if he went off presently to a museum and tried to apply his test to the pre-historic men on view there, it would fail for the simple reason that long ago they left their skins behind them. He would have to get to work, therefore, on their bony parts, and doubtless would attack the skulls for choice. By considering head-form and colour, then, we may help to cover a certain amount of the ground, vast as it is. For remember that anthropology in this department draws no line between ancient and modern, or between savage and civilized, but tries to tackle every sort of man that comes within its reach.

Head-shape is really a far more complicated thing to arrive at for purposes of comparison than one might suppose. Since no part of the skull maintains a stable position in regard to the rest, there can be no fixed standard of measurement, but at most a judgment of likeness or unlikeness founded on an averaging of the total proportions. Thus it comes about that, in the last resort, the impression of a good expert is worth in these matters a great deal more than rows of figures. Moreover, rows of figures in their turn take a lot of understanding. Besides, they are not always easy to get. This is especially the case if you are measuring a live subject. Perhaps he is armed with a club, and may take amiss the use of an instrument that has to be poked into his ears, or what not. So, for one reason or another, we have often to put up with that very unsatisfactory single-figure description of the head-form which is known as the cranial index. You take the greatest length and greatest breadth of the skull, and write down the result obtained by dividing the former into the latter when multiplied by 100. Medium-headed people have an index of anything between 75 and 80. Below that figure men rank as long-headed, above it as round-headed. This test, however, will not by itself carry us far. On the other hand, a good judge of head-form in all its aspects taken together will generally be able to make a pretty shrewd guess as to the people amongst whom the owner of a given skull is to be placed.

Unfortunately, to say people is not to say race. It may be that a given people tend to have a characteristic head-form, not so much because they are of common breed, as because they are subjected after birth, or at any rate, after conception, to one and the same environment. Thus some careful observations made recently by Professor Boas on American immigrants from various parts of Europe seem to show that the new environment does in some unexplained way modify the head-form to a remarkable extent. For example, amongst the East European Jews the head of the European-born is shorter and wider than that of the American-born, the difference being even more marked in the second generation of the American-born. At the same time, other European nationalities exhibit changes of other kinds, all these changes, however, being in the direction of a convergence towards one and the same American type. How are we to explain these facts, supposing them to be corroborated by more extensive studies? It would seem that we must at any rate allow for a considerable plasticity in the head-form, whereby it is capable of undergoing decisive alteration under the influences of environment; not, of course, at any moment during life, but during those early days when the growth of the head is especially rapid. The further question whether such an acquired character can be transmitted we need not raise again. Before passing on, however, let this one word to the wise be uttered. If the skull can be so affected, then what about the brain inside it? If the hereditarily long-headed can change under suitable conditions, then what about the hereditarily short-witted?

It remains to say a word about the types of pre-historic men as judged by their bony remains and especially by their skulls. Naturally the subject bristles with uncertainties.

By itself stands the so-called Pithecanthropus (Ape-man) of Java, a regular "missing link." The top of the skull, several teeth, and a thigh-bone, found at a certain distance from each other, are all that we have of it or him. Dr. Dubois, their discoverer, has made out a fairly strong case for supposing that the geological stratum in which the remains occurred is Pliocene-that is to say, belongs to the Tertiary epoch, to which man has not yet been traced back with any strong probability.

It must remain, however, highly doubtful whether this is a proto-human being, or merely an ape of a type related to the gibbon. The intermediate character is shown especially in the head form. If an ape, Pithecanthropus had an enormous brain; if a man, he must have verged on what we should consider idiocy.

Also standing somewhat by itself is the Heidelberg man. All that we have of him is a well-preserved lower jaw with its teeth. It was found more than eighty feet below the surface of the soil, in company with animal remains that make it possible to fix its position in the scale of pre-historic periods with some accuracy. Judged by this test, it is as old as the oldest of the unmistakable drift implements, the so-called Chellean (from Chelles in the department of Seine-et-Marne in France). The jaw by itself would suggest a gorilla, being both chinless and immensely powerful. The teeth, however, are human beyond question, and can be matched, or perhaps even in respect to certain marks of primitiveness out-matched, amongst ancient skulls of the Neanderthal order, if not also amongst modern ones from Australia.

We may next consider the Neanderthal group of skulls, so named after the first of that type found in 1856 in the Neanderthal valley close to Dusseldorf in the Rhine basin. A narrow head, with low and retreating forehead, and a thick projecting brow-ridge, yet with at least twice the brain capacity of any gorilla, set the learned world disputing whether this was an ape, a normal man, or an idiot. It was unfortunate that there were no proofs to hand of the age of these relics. After a while, however, similar specimens began to come in. Thus in 1866 the jaw of a woman, displaying a tendency to chinlessness combined with great strength, was found in the Cave of La Naulette in Belgium, associated with more or less dateable remains of the mammoth, woolly rhinoceros and reindeer. A few years earlier, though its importance was not appreciated at the moment, there had been discovered, near Forbes' quarry at Gibraltar, the famous Gibraltar skull, now to be seen in the Museum of the Royal College of Surgeons in London. Any visitor will notice at the first glance that this is no man of today. There are the narrow head, low crown, and prominent brow-ridge as before, supplemented by the most extraordinary eye-holes that were ever seen, vast circles widely separated from each other. And other peculiar features will reveal themselves on a close inspection; for instance, the horseshoe form in which, ape-fashion, the teeth are arranged, and the muzzle-like shape of the face due to the absence of the depressions that in our own case run down on each side from just outside the nostrils towards the corners of the mouth.

And now at the present time we have twenty or more individuals of this Neanderthal type to compare. The latest discoveries are perhaps the most interesting, because in two and perhaps other cases the man has been properly buried. Thus at La Chapelle-aux-Saints, in the French department of Correze, a skeleton, which in its head-form closely recalls the Gibraltar example, was found in a pit dug in the floor of a low grotto. It lay on its back, head to the west, with one arm bent towards the head, the other outstretched, and the legs drawn up. Some bison bones lay in the grave as if a food-offering had been made. Hard by were flint implements of a well-marked Mousterian type. In the shelter of Le Moustier itself a similar burial was discovered. The body lay on its right side, with the right arm bent so as to support the head upon a carefully arranged pillow of flints; whilst the left arm was stretched out, so that the hand might be near a magnificent oval stone-weapon chipped on both faces, evidently laid there by design. So much for these men of the Neanderthal type, denizens of the mid-palaeolithic world at the very latest. Ape-like they doubtless are in their head-form up to a certain point, though almost all their separate features occur here and there amongst modern Australian natives. And yet they were men enough, had brains enough, to believe in a life after death. There is something to think about in that.

Without going outside Europe, we have, however, to reckon with at least two other types of very early head-form. In one of the caves of Mentone known as La Grotte des Enfants two skeletons from a low stratum were of a primitive type, but unlike the Neanderthal, and have been thought to show affinities to the modern negro. As, however, no other Proto-Negroes are indisputably forthcoming either from Europe or from any other part of the world, there is little at present to be made out about this interesting racial type. In the layer immediately above the negroid remains, however, as well as in other caves at Mentone, were the bones of individuals of quite another order, one being positively a giant. They are known as the Cro-Magnon race, after a group of them discovered in a rock shelter of that name on the banks of the Vezere. These particular people can be shown to be Aurignacian-that is to say, to have lived just after the Mousterian men of the Neanderthal head-form. If, however, as has been already suggested, the Galley Hill individual, who shows affinities to the Cro-Magnon type, really goes back to the drift-period, then we can believe that from very early times there co-existed in Europe at least two varieties; and these so distinct, that some authorities would trace the original divergence between them right back to the times before man and the apes had parted company, linking the Neanderthal race with the gorilla and the Cro-Magnon race with the orang.

The Cro-Magnon head-form is refined and highly developed. The forehead is high, and the chin shapely, whilst neither the brow-ridge nor the lower jaw protrudes as in the Neanderthal type. Whether this race survives in modern Europe is, as was said in the last chapter, highly uncertain. In certain respects-for instance, in a certain shortness of face-these people present exceptional features; though some think they can still find men of this type in the Dordogne district. Perhaps the chances are, however, considering how skulls of the neolithic period prove to be anything but uniform, and suggest crossings between different stocks, that we may claim kinship to some extent with the more good-looking of the two main types of palaeolithic man-always supposing that head-form can be taken as a guide. But can it? The Pygmies of the Congo region have medium heads; the Bushmen of South Africa, usually regarded as akin in race, have long heads. The American Indians, generally supposed to be all, or nearly all, of one racial type, show considerable differences of head-form; and so on. It need not be repeated that any race-mark is liable to deceive.

We have sufficiently considered the use to which the particular race-mark of head-form has been put in the attempted classification of the very early men who have left their bones behind them. Let us now turn to another race-mark, namely colour; because, though it may really be less satisfactory than others, for instance hair, that is the one to which ordinary people naturally turn when they seek to classify by races the present inhabitants of the earth.

When Linnaeus in pre-Darwinian days distinguished four varieties of man, the white European, the red American, the yellow Asiatic, and the black African, he did not dream of providing the basis of anything more than an artificial classification. He probably would have agreed with Buffon in saying that in every case it was one and the same kind of man, only dyed differently by the different climates. But the Darwinian is searching for a natural classification. He wants to distinguish men according to their actual descent. Now race and descent mean for him the same thing. Hence a race-mark, if one is to be found, must stand for, by co-existing with, the whole mass of properties that form the inheritance. Can colour serve for a race-mark in this profound sense? That is the only question here.

First of all, what is the use of being coloured one way or the other? Does it make any difference? Is it something, like the heart-line of the hand, that may go along with useful qualities, but in itself seems to be a meaningless accident? Well, as some unfortunate people will be able to tell you, colour is still a formidable handicap in the struggle for existence. Not to consider the colour-prejudice in other aspects, there is no gainsaying the part it plays in sexual selection at this hour. The lower animals appear to be guided in the choice of a mate by externals of a striking and obvious sort. And men and women to this day marry more with their eyes than with their heads.

The coloration of man, however, though it may have come to subserve the purposes of mating, does not seem in its origin to have been like the bright coloration of the male bird. It was not something wholly useless save as a means of sexual attraction, though in such a capacity useful because a mark of vital vigour. Colour almost certainly developed in strict relation to climate. Right away in the back ages we must place what Bagehot has called the race-making epoch, when the chief bodily differences, including differences of colour, arose amongst men. In those days, we may suppose, natural selection acted largely on the body, because mind had not yet become the prime condition of survival. The rest is a question of pre-historic geography. Within the tropics, the habitat of the man-like apes, and presumably of the earliest men, a black skin protects against sunlight. A white skin, on the other hand-though this is more doubtful-perhaps economizes sun-heat in colder latitudes. Brown, yellow and the so-called red are intermediate tints suitable to intermediate regions. It is not hard to plot out in the pre-historic map of the world geographical provinces, or "areas of characterization," where races of different shades corresponding to differences in the climate might develop, in an isolation more or less complete, such as must tend to reinforce the process of differentiation.

Let it not be forgotten, however, that individual plasticity plays its part too in the determination of human colour. The Anglo-Indian planter is apt to return from a long sojourn in the East with his skin charged with a dark pigment which no amount of Pears' soap will remove during the rest of his life. It would be interesting to conduct experiments, on the lines of those of Professor Boas already mentioned, with the object of discovering in what degree the same capacity for amassing protective pigment declares itself in children of European parentage born in the tropics or transplanted thither during infancy. Correspondingly, the tendency of dark stocks to bleach in cold countries needs to be studied. In the background, too, lurks the question whether such effects of individual plasticity can be transmitted to offspring, and become part of the inheritance.

One more remark upon the subject of colour. Now-a-days civilized peoples, as well as many of the ruder races that the former govern, wear clothes. In other words they have dodged the sun, by developing, with the aid of mind, a complex society that includes the makers of white drill suits and solar helmets. But, under such conditions, the colour of one's skin becomes more or less of a luxury. Protective pigment, at any rate now-a-days, counts for little as compared with capacity for social service. Colour, in short, is rapidly losing its vital function. Will it therefore tend to disappear? In the long run, it would seem-perhaps only in the very long run-it will become dissociated from that general fitness to survive under particular climatic conditions of which it was once the innate mark. Be this as it may, race-prejudice, that is so largely founded on sheer considerations of colour, is bound to decay, if and when the races of darker colour succeed in displaying, on the average, such qualities of mind as will enable them to compete with the whites on equal terms, in a world which is coming more and more to include all climates.

Race and the Mental Aspect

Indeed, mind and plasticity are almost the same thing. Race, therefore, as being the stiffening in the evolution of life, might seem by its very nature opposed to mind as a limiting or obstructing force. Are we, then, going to return to the old pre-scientific notion of soul as something alien to body, and thereby simply clogged, thwarted and dragged down? That would never do. Body and soul are, for the working purposes of science, to be conceived as in perfect accord, as co-helpers in the work of life, and as such subject to a common development. Heredity, then, must be assumed to apply to both equally. In proportion as there is plastic mind there will be plastic body.

Unfortunately, the most plastic part of body is likewise the hardest to observe, at any rate whilst it is alive, namely, the brain. No certain criterion of heredity, then, is likely to be available from this quarter. You will see it stated, for instance, that the size of the brain cavity will serve to mark off one race from another. This is extremely doubtful, to put it mildly. No doubt the average European shows some advantage in this respect as compared, say, with the Bushman. But then you have to write off so much for their respective types of body, a bigger body going in general with a bigger head, that in the end you find yourself comparing mere abstractions. Again, the European may be the first to cry off on the ground that comparisons are odious; for some specimens of Neanderthal man in sheer size of the brain cavity are said to give points to any of our modern poets and politicians. Clearly, then, something is wrong with this test. Nor, if the brain itself be examined after death, and the form and number of its convolutions compared, is this criterion of hereditary brain-power any more satisfactory. It might be possible in this way to detect the difference between an idiot and a person of normal intelligence, but not the difference between a fool and a genius.

We cross the uncertain line that divides the bodily from the mental when we subject the same problem of hereditary mental endowment to the methods of what is known as experimental psychology. Thus acuteness of sight, hearing, taste, smell and feeling are measured by various ingenious devices. Seeing what stories travellers bring back with them about the hawk-like vision of hunting races, one might suppose that such comparisons would be all in their favour. The Cambridge Expedition to Torres Straits, however, of which Dr. Haddon was the leader, included several well-trained psychologists, who devoted special attention to this subject; and their results show that the sensory powers of these rude folk were on the average much the same as those of Europeans. It is the hunter's experience only that enables him to sight the game at an immense distance. There are a great many more complicated tests of the same type designed to estimate the force of memory, attention, association, reasoning and other faculties that most people would regard as purely mental; whilst another set of such tests deals with reaction to stimulus, co-ordination between hand and eye, fatigue, tremor, and, most ingenious perhaps of all, emotional excitement as shown through the respiration-phenomena which as it were, mental and bodily at once and together. Unfortunately, psychology cannot distinguish in such cases between the effects of heredity and those of individual experience, whether it take the form of high culture or of a dissipated life. Indeed, the purely temporary condition of body and mind is apt to influence the results. A man has been up late, let us say, or has been for a long walk, or has missed a meal; obviously his reaction-times, his record for memory, and so on, will show a difference for the worse. Or, again, the subject may confront the experiment in very various moods. At one moment he may be full of vanity, anxious to show what superior qualities he possesses; whilst at another time he will be bored. Not to labour the point further, these methods, whatever they may become in the future, are at present unable to afford any criterion whatever of the mental ability that goes with race. They are fertile in statistics; but an interpretation of these statistics that furthers our purpose is still to seek.

But surely, it will be said, we can tell an instinct when we come across it, so uniform as it is, and so independent of the rest of the system. Not at all. For one thing, the idea that an instinct is apiece of mechanism, as fixed as fate, is quite out of fashion. It is now known to be highly plastic in many cases, to vary considerably in individuals, and to involve conscious processes, thought, feeling and will, at any rate of an elementary kind. Again, how are you going to isolate an instinct? Those few automatic responses to stimulation that appear shortly after birth, as, for instance, sucking, may perhaps be recognized, since parental training and experience in general are out of the question here. But what about the instinct or group of instincts answering to sex? This is latent until a stage of life when experience is already in full swing. Indeed, psychologists are still busy discussing whether man has very few instincts or whether, on the contrary, he appears to have few because he really has so many that, in practice, they keep interfering with one another all the time. In support of the latter view, it has been recently suggested by Mr. McDougall that the best test of the instincts that we have is to be found in the specific emotions. He believes that every instinctive process consists of an afferent part or message, a central part, and an efferent part or discharge. At its two ends the process is highly plastic. Message and discharge, to which thought and will correspond, are modified in their type as experience matures. The central part, on the other hand, to which emotion answers on the side of consciousness, remains for ever much the same. To fear, to wonder, to be angry, or disgusted, to be puffed up, or cast down, or to be affected with tenderness-all these feelings, argues Mr. McDougall, and various more complicated emotions arising out of their combinations with each other, are common to all men, and bespeak in them deep-seated tendencies to react on stimulation in relatively particular and definite ways.

Yet, granting this, do we thus reach a criterion whereby the different races of men are to be distinguished? Far from it. Nay, on the contrary, as judged simply by his emotions, man is very much alike everywhere, from China to Peru. They are all there in germ, though different customs and grades of culture tend to bring special types of feeling to the fore.

Indeed, a certain paradox is to be noted here. The Negro, one would naturally say, is in general more emotional than the white man. Yet some experiments conducted by Miss Kellor of Chicago on negresses and white women, by means of the test of the effects of emotion on respiration, brought out the former as decidedly the more stolid of the two. And, whatever be thought of the value of such methods of proof, certain it is that the observers of rude races incline to put down most of them as apathetic, when not tuned up to concert-pitch by a dance or other social event. It may well be, then, that it is not the hereditary temperament of the Negro, so much as the habit, which he shares with other peoples at the same level of culture, of living and acting in a crowd, that accounts for his apparent excitability. But after all, "mafficking" is not unknown in civilized countries. Thus the quest for a race-mark of a mental kind is barren once more.

What, then, you exclaim, is the outcome of this chapter of negatives? Is it driving at the universal equality and brotherhood of man? Or, on the contrary, does it hint at the need of a stern system of eugenics? I offer nothing in the way of a practical suggestion. I am merely trying to show that, considered anthropologically-that is to say, in terms of pure theory-race or breed remains something which we cannot at present isolate, though we believe it to be there. Practice, meanwhile, must wait on theory; mere prejudices, bad as they are, are hardly worse guides to action than premature exploitations of science.

As regards the universal brotherhood of man, the most that can be said is this: The old ideas about race as something hard and fast for all time are distinctly on the decline. Plasticity, or, in other words, the power of adaptation to environment, has to be admitted to a greater share in the moulding of mind, and even of body, than ever before. But how plasticity is related to race we do not yet know. It may be that use-inheritance somehow incorporates its effects in the offspring of the plastic parents. Or it may be simply that plasticity increases with inter-breeding on a wider basis. These problems have still to be solved.

As regards eugenics, there is no doubt that a vast and persistent elimination of lives goes on even in civilized countries. It has been calculated that, of every hundred English born alive, fifty do not survive to breed, and, of the remainder, half produce three-quarters of the next generation. But is the elimination selective? We can hardly doubt that it is to some extent. But what its results are - whether it mainly favours immunity from certain diseases, or the capacity for a sedentary life in a town atmosphere, or intelligence and capacity for social service-is largely matter of guesswork. How, then, can we say what is the type to breed from, even if we confine our attention to one country? If, on the other hand, we look farther afield, and study the results of race-mixture or "miscegenation," we but encounter fresh puzzles. That the half-breed is an unsatisfactory person may be true; and yet, until the conditions of his upbringing are somehow discounted, the race problem remains exactly where it was. Or, again, it may be true that miscegenation increases human fertility, as some hold; but, until it is shown that the increase of fertility does not merely result in flooding the world with inferior types, we are no nearer to a solution.

If, then, there is a practical moral to this chapter, it is merely this: to encourage anthropologists to press forward with their study of race; and in the meantime to do nothing rash.

ENVIRONMENT

When a child is born it has been subjected for some three-quarters of a year already to the influences of environment. Its race, indeed, was fixed once for all at the moment of conception. Yet that superadded measure of plasticity, which has to be treated as something apart from the racial factor, enables it to respond for good or for evil to the pre-natal-that is to say, maternal-environment. Thus we may easily fall into the mistake of supposing our race to be degenerate, when poor feeding and exposure to unhealthy surroundings on the part of the mothers are really responsible for the crop of weaklings that we deplore. And, in so far as it turns out to be so, social reformers ought to heave a sigh of relief. Why? Because to improve the race by way of eugenics, though doubtless feasible within limits, remains an unrealized possibility through our want of knowledge. On the other hand, to improve the physical environment is fairly straight-ahead work, once we can awake the public conscience to the need of undertaking this task for the benefit of all classes of the community alike. If civilized man wishes to boast of being clearly superior to the rest of his kind, it must be mainly in respect to his control over the physical environment. Whatever may have been the case in the past, it seems as true now-a-days to say that man makes his physical environment as that his physical environment makes him.

Even if this be granted, however, it remains the fact that our material circumstances in the widest sense of the term play a very decisive part in the shaping of our lives. Hence the importance of geographical studies as they bear on the subject of man. From the moment that a child is conceived, it is subjected to what it is now the fashion to call a "geographic control." Take the case of the child of English parents born in India. Clearly several factors will conspire to determine whether it lives or dies. For simplicity's sake let us treat them as three. First of all, there is the fact that the child belongs to a particular cultural group; in other words, that it has been born with a piece of paper in its mouth representing one share in the British Empire. Secondly, there is its race, involving, let us say, blue eyes and light hair, and a corresponding constitution. Thirdly, there is the climate and all that goes with it. Though in the first of these respects the white child is likely to be superior to the native, inasmuch as it will be tended with more careful regard to the laws of health; yet such disharmony prevails between the other two factors of race and climate, that it will almost certainly die, if it is not removed at a certain age from the country. Possibly the English could acclimatize themselves in India at the price of an immense toll of infant lives; but it is a price which they show no signs of being willing to pay.

GEOGRAPHIC CONTROL

Situation, race and culture-to reduce it to a problem of three terms only-which of the three, if any, in the long run controls the rest? Remember that the anthropologist is trying to be the historian of long perspective. History which counts by years, proto-history which counts by centuries, pre-history which counts by millenniums-he seeks to embrace them all. He sees the English in India, on the one hand, and in Australia on the other. Will the one invasion prove an incident, he asks, and the other an event, as judged by a history of long perspective? Or, again, there are whites and blacks and redskins in the southern portion of the United States of America, having at present little in common save a common climate. Different races, different cultures, a common geographical situation-what net result will these yield for the historian of patient, far-seeing anthropological outlook? Clearly there is here something worth the puzzling out. But we cannot expect to puzzle it out all at once.

In these days geography, in the form known as anthropogeography, is putting forth claims to be the leading branch of anthropology. And, doubtless, a thorough grounding in geography must henceforth be part of the anthropologist's equipment. The schools of Ratzel in Germany and Le Play in France are, however, fertile in generalizations that are far too pretty to be true. Like other specialists, they exaggerate the importance of their particular brand of work. The full meaning of life can never be expressed in terms of its material conditions. I confess that I am not deeply moved when Ratzel announces that man is a piece of the earth. Or when his admirers, anxious to improve on this, after distinguishing the atmosphere or air, the hydrosphere or water, the lithosphere or crust, and the centrosphere or interior mass, proceed to add that man is the most active portion of an intermittent biosphere, or living envelope of our planet, I cannot feel that the last word has been said about him.

M. Demolins, author of a very suggestive book, 'Comment la route cree le type social("How the road creates the social type") comments, "There exists," he says in his preface, "on the surface of the terrestrial globe an infinite variety of peoples. What is the cause that has created this variety? In general the reply is, Race. But race explains nothing; for it remains to discover what has produced the diversity of races. Race is not a cause; it is a consequence. The first and decisive cause of the diversity of peoples and of the diversity of races is the road that the peoples have followed. It is the road that creates the race, and that creates the social type." And he goes further: "If the history of humanity were to recommence, and the surface of the globe had not been transformed, this history would repeat itself in its main lines. There might well be secondary differences, for example, in certain manifestations of public life, in political revolutions, to which we assign far too great an importance; but the same roads would reproduce the same social types, and would impose on them the same essential characters."

There is no contending with a pious opinion, especially when it takes the form of an unverifiable prophecy. Let the level-headed anthropologist beware, however, lest he put all his eggs into one basket. Let him seek to give each factor in the problem its due. Race must count for something, or why do not the other animals take a leaf out of our book and build up rival civilizations on suitable sites? Why do men herd cattle, instead of the cattle herding the men? We are rational beings, in other words, because we have it in us to be rational beings. Again, culture, with the intelligence and choice it involves, counts for something too. It is easy to argue that, since there were the Asiatic steppes with the wild horses ready to hand in them, man was bound sooner or later to tame the horse and develop the characteristic culture of the nomad type. Yes, but why did man tame the horse later rather than sooner? And why did the American redskins never tame the bison, and adopt a pastoral life in their vast prairies? Or why do modern black folk and white folk alike in Africa fail to utilize the elephant? Is it because these things cannot be done, or because man has not found out how to do them?

When all allowances, however, are made for the exaggerations almost pardonable in a branch of science still engaged in pushing its way to the front, anthropo-geography remains a far-reaching method of historical study which the anthropologist has to learn how to use. To put it crudely, he must learn how to work all the time with a map of the earth at his elbow.

First of all, let him imagine his world of man stationary. Let him plot out in turn the distribution of heat, of moisture, of diseases, of vegetation, of food-animals, of the physical types of man, of density of population, of industries, of forms of government, of religions, of languages, and so on and so forth. How far do these different distributions bear each other out? He will find a number of things that go together in what will strike him as a natural way. For instance, all along the equator, whether in Africa or South America or Borneo, he will find them knocking off work in the middle of the day in order to take a siesta. On the other hand, other things will not agree so well. Thus, though all will be dark-skinned, the South Americans will be coppery, the Africans black, and the men of Borneo yellow.

Led on by such discrepancies, perhaps, he will want next to set his world of man in movement. He will thereupon perceive a circulation, so to speak, amongst the various peoples, suggestive of interrelations of a new type. Now so long as he is dealing in descriptions of a detached kind, concerning not merely the physical environment, but likewise the social adjustments more immediately corresponding thereto, he will be working at the geographical level. Directly it comes, however, to a generalized description or historical explanation, as when he seeks to show that here rather than there a civilization is likely to arise, geographical considerations proper will not suffice. Distribution is merely one aspect of evolution. Yet that it is a very important aspect will now be shown by a hasty survey of the world according to geographical regions.

Let us begin with Europe, so as to proceed gradually from the more known to the less known. Lecky has spoken of "the European epoch of the human mind." What is the geographical and physical theatre of that epoch? Firstly, there was the river-phase; next, the Mediterranean phase; lastly, the present-day Atlantic phase. Thus, to begin with, the valleys of the Nile and Euphrates were each the home of civilizations both magnificent and enduring. They did not spring up spontaneously, however. If the rivers helped man, man also helped the rivers by inventing systems of irrigation. Next, from Minoan days right on to the end of the Middle Ages, the Mediterranean basin was the focus of all the higher life in the world, if we put out of sight the civilizations of India and China, together with the lesser cultures of Peru and Mexico. I will consider this second phase especially, because it is particularly instructive from the geographical standpoint. Finally, since the time of the discovery of America, the sea-trade, first called into existence as a civilizing agent by Mediterranean conditions, has shifted its base to the Atlantic coast, and especially to that land of natural harbours, the British Isles. We must give up thinking in terms of an Eastern and Western Hemisphere. The true distinction, as applicable to modern times, is between a land-hemisphere, with the Atlantic coast of Europe as its centre, and a sea-hemisphere, roughly coinciding with the Pacific. The Pacific is truly an ocean; but the Atlantic is becoming more of a "herring-pond" every day.

Fixing our eyes, then, on the Mediterranean basin, with its Black Sea extension, it is easy to perceive that we have here a well-defined geographical province, capable of acting as an area of characterization as perhaps no other in the world, once its various peoples had the taste and ingenuity to intermingle freely by way of the sea. The first fact to note is the completeness of the ring-fence that shuts it in. From the Pyrenees right along to Ararat runs the great Alpine fold, like a ridge in a crumpled table-cloth; the Spanish Sierras and the Atlas continue the circle to the south-west; and the rest is desert. Next, the configuration of the coasts makes for intercourse by sea, especially on the northern side with its peninsulas and islands, the remains of a foundered and drowned mountain-country. This same configuration, considered in connection with the flora and fauna that are favoured by the climate, goes far to explain that discontinuity of the political life which encouraged independence whilst it prevented self-sufficiency. The forest-belt, owing to the dry summer, lay towards the snow-line, and below it a scrub-belt, yielding poor hunting, drove men to grow their corn and olives and vines in the least swampy of the lowlands, scattered like mere oases amongst the hills and promontories.

For a long time, then, man along the north coasts must have been oppressed rather than assisted by his environment. It made mass-movements impossible. Great waves of migration from the steppe-land to the northeast, or from the forest-land to the north-west, would thunder on the long mountain barrier, only to trickle across in rivulets and form little pools of humanity here and there. Petty feuds between plain, shore, and mountain, as in ancient Attica, would but accentuate the prevailing division. Contrariwise, on the southern side of the Mediterranean, where there was open, if largely desert, country, there would be room under primitive conditions for a homogeneous race to multiply. It is in North Africa that we must probably place the original hotbed of that Mediterranean race, slight and dark with oval heads and faces, who during the neolithic period colonized the opposite side of the Mediterranean, and threw out a wing along the warm Atlantic coast as far north as Scotland, as well as eastwards to the Upper Danube; whilst by way of south and east they certainly overran Egypt, Arabia, and Somaliland, with probable ramifications still farther in both directions. At last, however, in the eastern Mediterranean was learnt the lesson of the profits attending the sea-going life, and there began the true Mediterranean phase, which is essentially an era of sea-borne commerce. Then was the chance for the northern shore with its peninsular configuration. Carthage on the south shore must be regarded as a bold experiment that did not answer. The moral, then, would seem to be that the Mediterranean basin proved an ideal nursery for seamen; but only as soon as men were brave and clever enough to take to the sea. The geographical factor is at least partly consequence as well as cause.

Now let us proceed farther north into what was for the earlier Mediterranean folk the breeding-ground of barbarous outlanders, forming the chief menace to their circuit of settled civic life. It is necessary to regard northern Europe and northern Asia as forming one geographic province. Asia Minor, together with the Euphrates valley and with Arabia in a lesser degree, belongs to the Mediterranean area. India and China, with the south-eastern corner of Asia that lies between them, form another system that will be considered separately later on.

The Eurasian northland consists naturally, that is to say, where cultivation has not introduced changes, of four belts. First, to the southward, come the mountain ranges passing eastwards into high plateau. Then, north of this line, from the Lower Danube, as far as China, stretches a belt of grassland or steppe-country at a lower level, a belt which during the milder periods of the ice-age and immediately after it must have reached as far as the Atlantic. Then we find, still farther to the north, a forest belt, well developed in the Siberia of to-day. Lastly, on the verge of the Arctic sea stretches the tundra, the frozen soil of which is fertile in little else than the lichen known as reindeer moss, whilst to the west, as, for instance, in our islands, moors and bogs represent this zone of barren lands in a milder form.

The mountain belt is throughout its entire length the home of round-headed peoples, the so-called Alpine race, which is generally supposed to have originally come from the high plateau country of Asia. These round-headed men in western Europe appear where-ever there are hills, throwing out offshoots by way of the highlands of central France into Brittany, and even reaching the British Isles. Here they introduced the use of bronze (an invention possibly acquired by contact with Egyptians in the near East), though without leaving any marked traces of themselves amongst the permanent population. At the other end of Europe they affected Greece by way of a steady though limited infiltration; whilst in Asia Minor they issued forth from their hills as the formidable Hittites, the people, by the way, to whom the Jews are said to owe their characteristic, yet non-Semitic, noses. But are these round-heads all of one race? Professor Ridgeway has put forward a rather paradoxical theory to the effect that, just as the long-faced Boer horse soon evolved in the mountains of Basutoland into a round-headed pony, so it is in a few generations with human mountaineers, irrespective of their breed. This is almost certainly to overrate the effects of environment. At the same time, in the present state of our knowledge, it would be premature either to affirm or deny that in the very long run round-headedness goes with a mountain life.

The grassland next claims our attention. Here is the paradise of the horse, and consequently of the horse-breaker. Hence, therefore, came the charging multitudes of Asiatic marauders who, after many repulses, broke through the Mediterranean cordon, and established themselves as the modern Turks; whilst at the other end of their beat they poured into China, which no great wall could avail to save, and established the Manchu domination. Given the steppe-country and a horse-taming people, we might seek, with the anthropo-geographers of the bolder sort, to deduce the whole way of life, the nomadism, the ample food, including the milk-diet infants need and find so hard to obtain farther south, the communal system, the patriarchal type of authority, the caravan-system that can set the whole horde moving along like a swarm of locusts, and so on. But, as has been already pointed out, the horse had to be tamed first. Palaeolithic man in western Europe had horse-meat in abundance. At Solutre, a little north of Lyons, a heap of food-refuse 100 yards long and 10 feet high largely consists of the bones of horses, most of them young and tender. This shows that the old hunters knew how to enjoy the passing hour in their improvident way, like the equally reckless Bushmen, who have left similar Golgothas behind them in South Africa. Yet apparently palaeolithic man did not tame the horse. Environment, in fact, can only give the hint; and man may not be ready to take it.

The forest-land of the north affords fair hunting in its way, but it is doubtful if it is fitted to rear a copious brood of men, at any rate so long as stone weapons are alone available wherewith to master the vegetation and effect clearings, whilst burning the brushwood down is precluded by the damp. Where the original home may have been of the so-called Nordic race, the large-limbed fair men of the Teutonic world, remains something of a mystery; though it is now the fashion to place it in the north-east of Europe rather than in Asia, and to suppose it to have been more or less isolated from the rest of the world by formerly existing sheets of water. Where-ever it was, there must have been grassland enough to permit of pastoral habits, modified, perhaps, by some hunting on the one hand, and by some primitive agriculture on the other. The Mediterranean men, coming from North Africa, an excellent country for the horse, may have vied with the Asiatics of the steppes in introducing a varied culture to the north. At any rate, when the Germans of Tacitus emerge into the light of history, they are not mere foresters, but rather woodlanders, men of the glades, with many sides to their life; including an acquaintance with the sea and its ways, surpassing by far that of those early beachcombers whose miserable kitchen-middens are to be found along the coast of Denmark.

Of the tundra it is enough to say that all depends on the reindeer. This animal is the be-all and end-all of Lapp existence. When Nansen, after crossing Greenland, sailed home with his two Lapps, he called their attention to the crowds of people assembled to welcome them at the harbour. "Ah," said the elder and more thoughtful of the pair, "if they were only reindeer!" When domesticated, the reindeer yields milk as well as food, though large numbers are needed to keep the community in comfort. Otherwise hunting and fishing must serve to eke out the larder. Miserable indeed are the tribes or rather remnants of tribes along the Siberian tundra who have no reindeer. On the other hand, if there are plenty of wild reindeer, as amongst the Koryaks and some of the Chukchis, hunting by itself suffices.

Let us now pass on from the Eurasian northland to what is, zoologically, almost its annexe, North America; its tundra, for example, where the Eskimo live, being strictly continuous with the Asiatic zone. Though having a very different fauna and flora, South America presumably forms part of the same geographical province so far as man is concerned, though there is evidence for thinking that he reached it very early. Until, however, more data are available for the pre-history of the American Indian, the great moulding forces, geographical or other, must be merely guessed at. Much turns on the period assigned to the first appearance of man in this region; for that he is indigenous is highly improbable, if only because no anthropoid apes are found here. The racial type, which, with the exception of the Eskimo, and possibly of the salmon-fishing tribes along the north-west coast, is one for the whole continent, has a rather distant resemblance to that of the Asiatic Mongols. Nor is there an difficulty in finding the immigrants a means of transit from northern Asia. Even if it be held that the land-bridge by way of what are now the Aleutian Islands was closed at too early a date for man to profit by it, there is always the passage over the ice by way of Behring Straits; which, if it bore the mammoth, as is proved by its remains in Alaska, could certainly bear man.

Once man was across, what was the manner of his distribution? On this point geography can at present tell us little. M. Demolins, it is true, describes three routes, one along the Rockies, the next down the central zone of prairies, and the third and most easterly by way of the great lakes. But this is pure hypothesis. No facts are adduced. Indeed, evidence bearing on distribution is very hard to obtain in this area, since the physical type is so uniform throughout. The best available criterion is the somewhat poor one of the distribution of the very various languages. Some curious lines of migration are indicated by the occurrence of the same type of language in widely separated regions, the most striking example being the appearance of one linguistic stock, the so-called Athapascan, away up in the north-west by the Alaska boundary; at one or two points in south-western Oregon and north-western California, where an absolute medley of languages prevails; and again in the southern highlands along the line of Colorado and Utah to the other side of the Mexican frontier. Does it follow from this distribution that the Apaches, at the southern end of the range, have come down from Alaska, by way of the Rockies and the Pacific slope, to their present habitat? It might be so in this particular case; but there are also those who think that the signs in general point to a northward dispersal of tribes, who before had been driven south by a period of glaciation. Thus the first thing to be settled is the antiquity of the American type of man.

A glance at South America must suffice. Geographically it consists of three regions. Westwards we have the Pacific line of bracing highlands, running down from Mexico as far as Chile, the home of two or more cultures of a rather high order. Then to the east there is the steaming equatorial forest, first covering a fan of rivers, then rising up into healthier hill-country, the whole in its wild state hampering to human enterprise. And below it occurs the grassland of the pampas, only needing the horse to bring out the powers of its native occupants.

Before leaving this subject of the domesticated horse, of which so much use has already been made in order to illustrate how geographic opportunity and human contrivance must help each other out, it is worth noticing how an invention can quickly revolutionize even that cultural life of the ruder races which is usually supposed to be quite hide-bound by immemorial custom. When the Europeans first broke in upon the redskins of North America, they found them a people of hunters and fishers, it is true, but with agriculture as a second string everywhere east of the Mississippi as well as to the south, and on the whole sedentary, with villages scattered far apart; so that in pre-Conquest days they would seem to have been enjoying a large measure of security and peace. The coming of the whites soon crowded them back upon themselves, disarranging the old boundaries. At the same time the horse and the gun were introduced. With extraordinary rapidity the Indian adapted himself to a new mode of existence, a grassland life, complicated by the fact that the relentless pressure of the invaders gave it a predatory turn which it might otherwise have lacked. Something very similar, though neither conditions nor consequences were quite the same, occurred in the pampas of South America, where horse-Indians like the Patagonians, who seem at first sight the indigenous outcrop of the very soil, are really the recent by-product of an intrusive culture.

And now let us hark back to southern Asia with its two reservoirs of life, India and China, and between them a jutting promontory pointing the way to the Indonesian archipelago, and thence onward farther still to the wide-flung Austral region with its myriad lands ranging in size from a continent to a coral-atoll. Here we have a nursery of seamen on a vaster scale than in the Mediterranean; for remember that from this point man spread, by way of the sea, from Easter Island in the Eastern Pacific right away to Madagascar, where we find Javanese immigrants, and negroes who are probably Papuan, whilst the language is of a Malayo-Polynesian type.

India and China each well-nigh deserve the status of geographical provinces on their own account. Each is an area of settlement; and, once there is settlement, there is a cultural influence which co-operates with the environment to weed out immigrant forms; as we see, for example, in Egypt, where a characteristic physical type, or rather pair of types, a coarser and a finer, has apparently persisted, despite the constant influx of other races, from the dawn of its long history. India, however, and China have both suffered so much invasion from the Eurasian northland, and at the same time are of such great extent and comprise such diverse physical conditions, that they have, in the course of the long years, sent forth very various broods of men to seek their fortunes in the south-east.

Nor must we ignore the possibility of an earlier movement in the opposite direction. In Indonesia, the home of the orangutan and gibbon, not to speak of Pithecanthropus, many authorities would place the original home of the human race. It will be wise to touch lightly on matters involving considerations of palaeo-geography, that most kaleidoscopic of studies. The submerged continents which it calls from the vasty deep have a habit of crumbling away again. Let us therefore refrain from providing man with land-bridges (draw-bridges, they might almost be called), whether between the Indonesian islands; or between New Guinea, Australia and Tasmania; or between Indonesia and Africa by way of the Indian Ocean. Let the curious facts about the present distribution of the racial types speak for themselves, the difficulties about identifying a racial type being in the meantime ever borne in mind.

Most striking of all is the diffusion of the Negro stocks with black skin and woolly hair. Their range is certainly suggestive of a breeding-ground somewhere about Indonesia. To the extreme west are the negroes of Africa, to the extreme east the Papuasians (Papuans and Melanesians) extending from New Guinea through the oceanic islands as far as Fiji. A series of connecting links is afforded by the small negroes of the pygmy type, the so-called Negritos. It is not known how far they represent a distinct and perhaps earlier experiment in negro-making, though this is the prevailing view; or whether the negro type, with its tendency to infantile characters due to the early closing of the cranial sutures, is apt to throw off dwarfed forms in an occasional way. At any rate, in Africa there are several groups of pygmies in the Congo region, as well as the Bushmen and allied stocks in South Africa. Then the Andaman Islanders, the Semang of the Malay Peninsula, the Aket of eastern Sumatra, the now extinct Kalangs of Java, said to have been in some respects the most ape-like of human beings, the Aetas of the Philippines, and the dwarfs, with a surprisingly high culture, recently reported from Dutch New Guinea, are like so many scattered pieces of human wreckage. Finally, if we turn our gaze southward, we find that Negritos until the other day inhabited Tasmania; whilst in Australia a strain of Negrito, or Negro (Papuan), blood is likewise to be detected.

Are we here on the track of the original dispersal of man? It is impossible to say. It is not even certain, though highly probable, that man originated in one spot. If he did, he must have been hereditarily endowed, almost from the outset, with an adaptability to different climates quite unique in its way. The tiger is able to range from the hot Indian jungle to the freezing Siberian tundra; but man is the cosmopolitan animal beyond all others. Somehow, on this theory of a single origin, he made his way to every quarter of the globe; and when he got there, though needing time, perhaps, to acquire the local colour, managed in the end to be at home. It looks as if both race and a dash of culture had a good deal to do with his exploitation of geographical opportunity. How did the Australians and their Negrito forerunners invade their Austral world, at some period which, we cannot but suspect, was immensely remote in time? Certain at least it is that they crossed a formidable barrier. What is known as Wallace's line corresponds with the deep channel running between the islands of Bali and Lombok and continuing northwards to the west of Celebes. On the eastern side the fauna are non-Asiatic. Yet somehow into Australia with its queer monotremes and marsupials entered triumphant man-man and the dog with him. Haeckel has suggested that man followed the dog, playing as it were the jackal to him. But this sounds rather absurd. It looks as if man had already acquired enough seamanship to ferry himself across the zoological divide, and to take his faithful dog with him on board his raft or dug-out. Until we have facts whereon to build, however, it would be as unpardonable to lay down the law on these matters as it is permissible to fill up the blank by guesswork.

It remains to round off our original survey by a word or two more about the farther extremities, west, south, and east, of this vast southern world, to which south-eastern Asia furnishes a natural approach. The negroes did not have Africa, that is, Africa south of the Sahara, all to themselves. In and near the equatorial forest-region of the west the pure type prevails, displaying agricultural pursuits such as the cultivation of the banana, and, farther north, of millet, that must have been acquired before the race was driven out of the more open country. Elsewhere occur mixtures of every kind with intrusive pastoral peoples of the Mediterranean type, the negro blood, however, tending to predominate; and thus we get the Fulahs and similar stocks to the west along the grassland bordering on the desert; the Nilotic folk amongst the swamps of the Upper Nile; and throughout the eastern and southern parkland the vigorous Bantu peoples, who have swept the Bushmen and the kindred Hottentots before them down into the desert country in the extreme south-west. It may be added that Africa has a rich fauna and flora, much mineral wealth, and a physical configuration that, in respect to its interior, though not to its coasts, is highly diversified; so that it may be doubted whether the natives have reached as high a pitch of indigenous culture as the resources of the environment, considered by itself, might seem to warrant. If the use of iron was invented in Africa, as some believe, it would only be another proof that opportunity is nothing apart from the capacity to grasp it.

Of the Australian aborigines something has been said already. Apart from the Negrito or Negro strain in their blood, they are usually held to belong to that pre-Dravidian stock represented by various jungle tribes in southern India and by the Veddas of Ceylon, connecting links between the two areas being the Sakai of the Malay Peninsula and East Sumatra, and the Toala of Celebes. It may be worth observing, also, that pre-historic skulls of the Neanderthal type find their nearest parallels in modern Australia. We are here in the presence of some very ancient dispersal, from what centre and in what direction it is hard to imagine. In Australia these early colonists found pleasant, if somewhat lightly furnished, lodgings. In particular there were no dangerous beasts; so that hunting was hardly calculated to put a man on his mettle, as in more exacting climes.

Isolation, and the consequent absence of pressure from human intruders, is another fact in the situation. Whatever the causes, the net result was that, despite a very fair environment, away from the desert regions of the interior, man on the whole stagnated. In regard to material comforts and conveniences, the rudeness of their life seems to us appalling. On the other hand, now that we are coming to know something of the inner life and mental history of the Australians, a somewhat different complexion is put upon the state of their culture. With very plain living went something that approached to high thinking; and we must recognize in this case, as in others, what might be termed a differential evolution of culture, according to which some elements may advance, whilst others stand still, or even decay.

To another and a very different people, namely, the Polynesians, the same notion of a differential evolution may be profitably applied. They were in the stone-age when first discovered, and had no bows and arrows. On the other hand, with coconut, bananas and bread-fruit, they had abundant means of sustenance, and were thoroughly at home in their magnificent canoes. Thus their island-life was rich in ease and variety; and, whilst rude in certain respects, they were almost civilized in others. Their racial affinities are somewhat complex. What is almost certain is that they only occupied the Eastern Pacific during the course of the last 1500 years or so. They probably came from Indonesia, mixing to a slight extent with Melanesians on their way. How the proto-Polynesians came into existence in Indonesia is more problematic. Possibly they were the result of a mixture between long-headed immigrants from eastern India, and round-headed Mongols from Indo-China and the rest of south-eastern Asia, from whom the present Malays are derived.

We have completed our very rapid regional survey of the world; and what do we find? By no means is it case after case of one region corresponding to one type of man and to one type of culture. It might be that, given persistent physical conditions of a uniform kind, and complete isolation, human life would in the end conform to these conditions, or in other words stagnate. No one can tell, and no one wants to know, because as a matter of fact no such environmental conditions occur in this world of ours. Human history reveals itself as a bewildering series of interpenetrations. What excites these movements? Geographical causes, say the theorists of one idea. No doubt man moves forward partly because nature kicks him behind. But in the first place some types of animal life go forward under pressure from nature, whilst others lie down and die. In the second place man has an accumulative faculty, a social memory, whereby he is able to carry on to the conquest of a new environment whatever has served him in the old. But this is as it were to compound environments-a process that ends by making the environment coextensive with the world. Intelligent assimilation of the new by means of the old breaks down the provincial barriers one by one, until man, the cosmopolitan animal by reason of his hereditary constitution, develops a cosmopolitan culture; at first almost unconsciously, but later on with self-conscious intent, because he is no longer content to live, but insists on living well.

As a sequel to this brief examination of the geographic control considered by itself it would be interesting, if space allowed, to append a study of the distribution of the arts and crafts of a more obviously economic and utilitarian type. If the physical environment were all in all, we ought to find the same conditions evoking the same industrial appliances everywhere, without the aid of suggestions from other quarters. Indeed, so little do we know about the conditions attending the discovery of the arts of life that gave humanity its all-important start-the making of fire, the taming of animals, the sowing of plants, and so on-that it is only too easy to misread our map. We know almost nothing of those movements of peoples, in the course of which a given art was brought from one part of the world to another. Hence, when we find the art duly installed in a particular place, and utilizing the local product, the bamboo in the south, let us say, or the birch in the north, as it naturally does, we easily slip into the error of supposing that the local products of themselves called the art into existence. Similar needs, we say, have generated similar expedients. No doubt there is some truth in this principle; but I doubt if, on the whole, history tends to repeat itself in the case of the great useful inventions. We are all of us born imitators, but inventive genius is rare.

Take the case of the early palaeoliths of the drift type. From Egypt, Somaliland, and many other distant lands come examples which Sir John Evans finds "so identical in form and character with British specimens that they might have been manufactured by the same hands." And throughout the palaeolithic age in Europe the very limited number and regular succession of forms testifies to the innate conservatism of man, and the slow progress of invention. And yet, as some American writers have argued-who do not find that the distinction between chipped palaeoliths and polished neoliths of an altogether later age applies equally well to the New World-it was just as easy to have got an edge by rubbing as by flaking. The fact remains that in the Old World human inventiveness moved along one channel rather than another, and for an immense lapse of time no one was found to strike out a new line. There was plenty of sand and water for polishing, but it did not occur to their minds to use it.

As regards its uses in the rest of the world, it may be said at once that here and there, in Galicia in Europe, in the Malay Peninsula in Asia, and amongst the Bushmen in Africa, it is used to drive or scare animals, whether tame or wild. And this, to make a mere guess, may have been its earliest use, if utilitarian contrivances can generally claim historical precedence, as is by no means certain. As long as man hunted with very inferior weapons, he must have depended a good deal on drives, that either forced the game into a pitfall, or rounded them up so as to enable a concerted attack to be made by the human pack. No wonder that the bull-roarer is sometimes used to bring luck in a mystic way to hunters. More commonly, however, at the present day, the bull-roarer serves another type of mystic purpose, its noise, which is so suggestive of thunder or wind, with a superadded touch of weirdness and general mystery, fitting it to play a leading part in rain-making ceremonies. From these not improbably have developed all sorts of other ceremonies connected with making vegetation and the crops grow, and with making the boys grow into men, as is done at the initiation rites. It is not surprising, therefore, to find a carved human face appearing on the bull-roarer in New Guinea, and again away in North America, whilst in West Africa it is held to contain the voice of a very god. In Australia, too, all their higher notions about a benevolent deity and about religious matters in general seem to concentrate on this strange symbol, outwardly the frailest of toys, yet to the spiritual eye of these simple folk a veritable holy of holies.

And now for the merest sketch of its distribution, the details of which are to be learnt from Dr. Haddon's valuable paper in 'The Study of Man'. England, Scotland, Ireland and Wales have it. It can be tracked along central Europe through Switzerland, Germany, and Poland beyond the Carpathians, whereupon ancient Greece with its Dionysiac mysteries takes up the tale. In America it is found amongst the Eskimo, is scattered over the northern part of the continent down to the Mexican frontier, and then turns up afresh in central Brazil. Again, from the Malay Peninsula and Sumatra it extends over the great fan of darker peoples, from Africa, west and south, to New Guinea, Melanesia, and Australia, together with New Zealand alone of Polynesian islands - a fact possibly showing it to have belonged to some earlier race of colonists. Thus in all of the great geographical areas the bull-roarer is found, and that without reckoning in analogous implements like the so-called "buzz," which cover further ground, for instance, the eastern coastlands of Asia. Are we to postulate many independent origins, or else far-reaching transportations by migratory peoples, by the American Indians and the negroes, for example? No attempt can be made here to answer these questions. It is enough to have shown by the use of a single illustration how the study of the geographical distribution of inventions raises as many difficulties as it solves.

Our conclusion, then, must be that the anthropologist, whilst constantly consulting his physical map of the world, must not suppose that by so doing he will be saved all further trouble. Geographical facts represent a passive condition, which life, something by its very nature active, obeys, yet in obeying conquers. We cannot get away from the fact that we are physically determined. Yet, physical determinations have been surmounted by human nature in a way to which the rest of the animal world affords no parallel. Thus man, as the old saying has it, makes love all the year round. Seasonal changes of course affect him, yet he is no slave of the seasons. And so it is with the many other elements involved in the "geographic control." The "road," for instance-that is to say, any natural avenue of migration or communication, whether by land over bridges and through passes, or by sea between harbours and with trade-winds to swell the sails-takes a hand in the game of life, and one that holds many trumps; but so again does the non-geographical fact that your travelling-machine may be your pair of legs, or a horse, or a boat, or a railway, or an airship. Let us be moderate in all things, then, even in our references to the force of circumstances. Circumstances can unmake; but of themselves they never yet made man, nor any other form of life.

6

Language and Social Change

The differentia of man-the quality that marks him off from the other animal kinds-is undoubtedly the power of articulate speech. Thereby his mind itself becomes articulate. If language is ultimately a creation of the intellect, yet hardly less fundamentally is the intellect a creation of language. As flesh depends on bone, so does the living tissue of our spiritual life depend on its supporting framework of steadfast verbal forms. The genius, the heaven-born benefactor of humanity, is essentially he who wrestles with "thoughts too deep for words," until at last he assimilates them to the scheme of meanings embodied in his mother-tongue, and thus raises them definitely above the threshold of the common consciousness, which is likewise the threshold of the common culture.

There is good reason, then, for prefixing a short chapter on language to an account of those factors in the life of man that together stand on the whole for the principle of freedom-of rational self-direction. Heredity and environment do not, indeed, lie utterly beyond the range of our control. As they are viewed from the standpoint of human history as a whole, they show each in its own fashion a certain capacity to meet the needs and purposes of the life-force halfway. Regarded abstractly, however, they may conveniently be treated as purely passive and limiting conditions. Here we are with a constitution not of our choosing, and in a world not of our choosing. Given this inheritance, and this environment, how are we, by taking thought and taking risks, to achieve the best-under-the-circumstances? Such is the vital problem as it presents itself to any particular generation of men.

The environment is as it were the enemy. We are out to conquer and enslave it. Our inheritance, on the other hand, is the impelling force we obey in setting forth to fight; it tingles in our blood, and nerves the muscles of our arm. This force of heredity, however, abstractly considered, is blind. Yet, corporately and individually, we fight with eyes that see. This supervening faculty, then, of utilizing the light of experience represents a third element in the situation; and, from the standpoint of man's desire to know himself, the supreme element. The environment, inasmuch as under this conception are included all other forms of life except man, can muster on its side a certain amount of intelligence of a low order. But man's prerogative is to dominate his world by the aid of intelligence of a high order. When he defied the ice-age by the use of fire, when he outfaced and outlived the mammoth and the cave bear, he was already the rational animal, 'homo sapiens'. In his way he thought, even in those far-off days. And therefore we may assume, until direct evidence is forthcoming to the contrary, that he likewise had language of an articulate kind. He tried to make a speech, we may almost say, as soon as he had learned to stand up on his hind legs.

Unfortunately, we entirely lack the means of carrying back the history of human speech to its first beginnings. In the latter half of the last century, whilst the ferment of Darwinism was freshly seething, all sorts of speculations were rife concerning the origin of language. One school sought the source of the earliest words in imitative sounds of the type of bow-wow; another in interjectional expressions of the type of tut-tut. Or, again, as was natural in Europe, where, with the exception of Basque in a corner of the west, and of certain Asiatic languages, Turkish, Hungarian and Finnish, on the eastern border, all spoken tongues present certain obvious affinities, the comparative philologist undertook to construct sundry great families of speech; and it was hoped that sooner or later, by working back to some linguistic parting of the ways, the central problem would be solved of the dispersal of the world's races.

These painted bubbles have burst. The further examination of the forms of speech current amongst peoples of rude culture has not revealed a conspicuous wealth either of imitative or of interjectional sounds. On the other hand, the comparative study of the European, or, as they must be termed in virtue of the branch stretching through Persia into India, the Indo-European stock of languages, carries us back three or four thousand years at most-a mere nothing in terms of anthropological time. Moreover, a more extended search through the world, which in many of its less cultured parts furnishes no literary remains that may serve to illustrate linguistic evolution, shows endless diversity of tongues in place of the hoped-for system of a few families; so that half a hundred apparently independent types must be distinguished in North America alone. For the rest, it has become increasingly clear that race and language need not go together at all. What philologist, for instance, could ever discover, if he had no history to help him, but must rely wholly on the examination of modern French, that the bulk of the population of France is connected by way of blood with ancient Gauls who spoke Celtic, until the Roman conquest caused them to adopt a vulgar form of Latin in its place. The Celtic tongue, in its turn, had, doubtless not so very long before, ousted some earlier type of language, perhaps one allied to the still surviving Basque; though it is not in the least necessary, therefore, to suppose that the Celtic-speaking invaders wiped out the previous inhabitants of the land to a corresponding extent. Races, in short, mix readily; languages, except in very special circumstances, hardly at all.

Disappointed in its hope of presiding over the reconstruction of the distant past of man, the study of language has in recent years tended somewhat to renounce the historical-that is to say, anthropological-method altogether. The alternative is a purely formal treatment of the subject. Thus, whereas vocabularies seem hopelessly divergent in their special contents, the general apparatus of vocal expression is broadly the same everywhere. That all men alike communicate by talking, other symbols and codes into which thoughts can be translated, such as gestures, the various kinds of writing, drum-taps, smoke signals, and so on, being in the main but secondary and derivative, is a fact of which the very universality may easily blind us to its profound significance. Meanwhile, the science of phonetics-having lost that "guid conceit of itself" which once led it to discuss at large whether the art of talking evolved at a single geographical centre, or at many centres owing to similar capacities of body and mind-contents itself now-a-days for the most part with conducting an analytic survey of the modes of vocal expression as correlated with the observed tendencies of the human speech-organs. And what is true of phonetics in particular is hardly less true of comparative philology as a whole. Its present procedure is in the main analytic or formal. Thus its fundamental distinction between isolating, agglutinative and inflectional languages is arrived at simply by contrasting the different ways in which words are affected by being put together into a sentence. No attempt is made to show that one type of arrangement normally precedes another in time, or that it is in any way more rudimentary-that is to say, less adapted to the needs of human intercourse. It is not even pretended that a given language is bound to exemplify one, and one alone, of these three types; though the process known as analogy-that is, the regularizing of exceptions by treating the unlike as if it were like-will always be apt to establish one system at the expense of the rest.

If, then, the study of language is to recover its old preeminence amongst anthropological studies, it looks as if a new direction must be given to its inquiries. And there is much to be said for any change that would bring about this result. Without constant help from the philologist, anthropology is bound to languish. To thoroughly understand the speech of the people under investigation is the field-worker's master-key; so much so, that the critic's first question in determining the value of an ethnographical work must always be, Could the author talk freely with the natives in their own tongue? But how is the study of particular languages to be pursued successfully, if it lack the stimulus and inspiration which only the search for general principles can impart to any branch of science? To relieve the hack-work of compiling vocabularies and grammars, there must be present a sense of wider issues involved, and such issues as may directly interest a student devoted to language for its own sake. The formal method of investigating language, in the meantime, can hardly supply the needed spur. Analysis is all very well so long as its ultimate purpose is to subserve genesis-that is to say, evolutionary history. If, however, it tries to set up on its own account, it is in danger of degenerating into sheer futility. Out of time and history is, in the long run, out of meaning and use. The philologist, then, if he is to help anthropology, must himself be an anthropologist, with a full appreciation of the importance of the historical method. He must be able to set each language or group of languages that he studies in its historical setting. He must seek to show how it has evolved in relation to the needs of a given time. In short, he must correlate words with thoughts; must treat language as a function of the social life.

CHARACTERISTICS OF LANGUAGE

It is not possible to attempt any but the most general characterization of primitive language as it throws light on the workings of the primitive intelligence. For one reason, the subject is highly technical; for another reason, our knowledge about most types of savage speech is backward in the extreme; whilst, for a third and most far-reaching reason of all, many peoples, as we have seen, are not speaking the language truly native to their powers and habits of mind, but are expressing themselves in terms imported from another stock, whose spiritual evolution has been largely different. Thus it is at most possible to contrast very broadly and generally the more rudimentary with the more advanced methods that mankind employs for the purpose of putting its experience into words. Happily the careful attention devoted by American philologists to the aboriginal languages of their continent has resulted in the discovery of certain principles which the rest of our evidence, so far as it goes, would seem to stamp as of world-wide application. The reader is advised to study the most stimulating, if perhaps somewhat speculative, pages on language in the second volume of E.J. Payne's 'History of the New World called America'; or, if he can wrestle with the French tongue, to compare the conclusions here reached with those to which Professor Levy-Bruhl is led, largely by the consideration of this same American group of languages, in his recent work, 'Les Fonctions Mentales dans les Societes Inferieures("Mental Functions in the Lower Societies").

If the average man who had not looked into the matter at all were asked to say what sort of language he imagined a savage to have, he would be pretty sure to reply that in the first place the vocabulary would be very small, and in the second place that it would consist of very short, comprehensive terms-roots, in fact-such as "man," "bear," "eat," "kill," and so on. Nothing of the sort is actually the case. Take the inhabitants of that cheerless spot, Tierra del Fuego, whose culture is as rude as that of any people on earth. A scholar who tried to put together a dictionary of their language found that he had got to reckon with more than thirty thousand words, even after suppressing a large number of forms of lesser importance. And no wonder that the tally mounted up. For the Fuegians had more than twenty words, some containing four syllables, to express what for us would be either "he" or "she"; then they had two names for the sun, two for the moon, and two more for the full moon, each of the last-named containing four syllables and having no element in common. Sounds, in fact, are with them as copious as ideas are rare. Impressions, on the other hand, are, of course, infinite in number. By means of more or less significant sounds, then, Fuegian society compounds impressions, and that somewhat imperfectly, rather than exchanges ideas, which alone are the currency of true thought.

For instance, I-cut-bear's-leg-at-the-joint-with-a-flint-now corresponds fairly well with the total impression produced by the particular act; though, even so, I have doubtless selectively reduced the notion to something I can comfortably take in, by leaving out a lot of unnecessary detail-for instance, that I was hungry, in a hurry, doing it for the benefit of others as well as myself, and so on. Well, American languages of the ruder sort, by running a great number of sounds or syllables together, manage to utter a portmanteau word-"holophrase" is the technical name for it-into which is packed away enough suggestions to reproduce the situation in all its detail, the cutting, the fact that I did it, the object, the instrument, the time of the cutting, and who knows what besides. Amusing examples of such portmanteau words meet one in all the text-books. To go back to the Fuegians, their expression 'mamihlapinatapaiis said to mean "to look at each other hoping that either will offer to do something which both parties desire but are unwilling to do." Now, since exactly the same situation never recurs, but is partly the same and partly different, it is clear that, if the holophrase really tried to hit off in each case the whole outstanding impression that a given situation provoked, then the same combination of sounds would never recur either; one could never open one's mouth without coining a new word. Ridiculous as this notion sounds, it may serve to mark a downward limit from which the rudest types of human speech are not so very far removed. Their well-known tendency to alter their whole character in twenty years or less is due largely to the fluid nature of primitive utterance; it being found hard to detach portions, capable of repeated use in an unchanged form, from the composite vocables wherein they register their highly concrete experiences.

Thus in the old Huron-Iroquois language 'eschoir-honmeans "I-have-been-to-the-water," 'setsanha"Go-to-the-water,"'ondequoha"There-is-water-in-the-bucket," 'daustantewacharet' "There-is-water-in-the-pot." In this case there is said to have been a common word for "water," 'awen', which, moreover, is somehow suggested to an aboriginal ear as an element contained in each of these longer forms. In many other cases the difficulty of isolating the common meaning, and fixing it by a common term, has proved too much altogether for a primitive language. You can express twenty different kinds of cutting; but you simply cannot say "cut" at all. No wonder that a large vocabulary is found necessary, when, as in Zulu, "my father," "thy father," "his-or-her-father," are separate polysyllables without any element in common.

The evolution of language, then, on this view, may be regarded as a movement out of, and away from, the holophrastic in the direction of the analytic. When every piece in your play-box of verbal bricks can be dealt with separately, because it is not joined on in all sorts of ways to the other pieces, then only can you compose new constructions to your liking. Order and emphasis, as is shown by English, and still more conspicuously by Chinese, suffice for sentence-building. Ideally, words should be individual and atomic. Every modification they suffer by internal change of sound, or by having prefixes or suffixes tacked on to them, involves a curtailment of their free use and a sacrifice of distinctness. It is quite easy, of course, to think confusedly, even whilst employing the clearest type of language; though in such a case it is very hard to do so without being quickly brought to book. On the other hand, it is not feasible to attain to a high degree of clear thinking, when the only method of speech available is one that tends towards wordlessness-that is to say, is relatively deficient in verbal forms that preserve their identity in all contexts. Wordless thinking is not in the strictest sense impossible; but its somewhat restricted opportunities lie almost wholly on the farther side, as it were, of a clean-cut vocabulary. For the very fact that the words are crystallized into permanent shape invests them with a suggestion of interrupted continuity, an overtone of un-utilized significance, that of itself invites the mind to play with the corresponding fringe of meaning attaching to the concepts that the words embody.

Person, number, case, tense, mood and gender-all these, even in the relatively analytical phraseology of the most cultured peoples, are apt to impress themselves on the very body of the words of which they qualify the sense. But the meagre list of determinations thus produced in an evolved type of language can yield one no idea of the vast medley of complicated forms that serve the same ends at the lower levels of human experience. Moreover, there are many other shades of secondary and circumstantial meaning which in advanced languages are invariably represented by distinct words, so that when not wanted they can be left out, but in a more primitive tongue are apt to run right through the very grammar of the sentence, thus mixing themselves up inextricably with the really substantial elements in the thought to be conveyed. For instance, in some American languages, things are either animate or inanimate, and must be distinguished accordingly by accompanying particles. Or, again, they are classed by similar means as rational or irrational; women, by the bye, being designated amongst the Chiquitos by the irrational sign. Reverential particles, again, are used to distinguish what is high or low in the tribal estimation; and we get in this connection such oddities as the Tamil practice of restricting the privilege of having a plural to high-caste names, such as those applied to gods and human beings, as distinguished from the beasts, which are mere casteless "things." Or, once more, my transferable belongings, "my-spear," or "my-canoe," undergo verbal modifications which are denied to non-transferable possessions such as "my-hand"; "my-child," be it observed, falling within the latter class.

Most interesting of all are distinctions of person. These cannot but bite into the forms of speech, since the native mind is taken up mostly with the personal aspect of things, attaining to the conception of a bloodless system of "its" with the greatest difficulty, if at all. Even the third person, which is naturally the most colourless, because excluded from a direct part of the conversational game, undergoes multitudinous leavening in the light of conditions which the primitive mind regards as highly important, whereas we should banish them from our thoughts as so much irrelevant "accident." Thus the Abipones in the first place distinguished "he-present," 'eneha', and "she-present," 'anaha', from "he-absent" and "she-absent." But presence by itself gave too little of the speaker's impression. So, if "he" or "she" were sitting, it was necessary to say 'hinihaand 'haneha'; if they were walking and in sight 'ehahaand 'ahaha', but, if walking and out of sight, 'ekahaand 'akaha'; if they were lying down, 'hirihaand 'haraha', and so on. Moreover, these were all "collective" forms, implying that there were others involved as well. If "he" or "she" were alone in the matter, an entirely different set of words was needed, "he-sitting (alone)" becoming 'ynitara', and so forth. The modest requirements of Fuegian intercourse have called more than twenty such separate pronouns into being.

Without attempting to go thoroughly into the efforts of primitive speech to curtail its interest in the personnel of its world by gradually acquiring a stock of de-individualized words, let us glance at another aspect of the subject, because it helps to bring out the fundamental fact that language is a social product, a means of intersubjective intercourse developed within a society that hands on to a new generation the verbal experiments that are found to succeed best. Payne shows reason for believing that the collective "we" precedes "I" in the order of linguistic evolution. To begin with, in America and elsewhere, "we" may be inclusive and mean "all-of-us," or selective, meaning "some-of-us-only." Hence, we are told, a missionary must be very careful, and, if he is preaching, must use the inclusive "we" in saying "we have sinned," lest the congregation assume that only the clergy have sinned; whereas, in praying, he must use the selective "we," or God would be included in the list of sinners. Similarly, "I" has a collective form amongst some American languages, and this is ordinarily employed, whereas the corresponding selective form is used only in special cases. Thus if the question be "Who will help?" the Apache will reply "I-amongst-others," "I-for-one"; but, if he were recounting his own personal exploits, he says 'sheedah', "I-by-myself," to show that they were wholly his own. Here we seem to have group-consciousness holding its own against individual self-consciousness, as being for primitive folk on the whole the more normal attitude of mind.

Another illustration of the sociality engrained in primitive speech is to be found in the terms employed to denote relationship. "My-mother," to the child of nature, is something more than an ordinary mother like yours. Thus, as we have already seen, there may be a special particle applying to blood-relations as non-transferable possessions. Or, again, one Australian language has special duals, "we-two," one to be used between relations generally, another between father and child only. Or an American language supplies one kind of plural suffix for blood-relations, another for the rest of human beings. These linguistic concretions are enough to show how hard it is for primitive thought to disjoin what is joined fast in the world of everyday experience.

No wonder that it is usually found impracticable by the European traveller who lacks an anthropological training to extract from natives any coherent account of their system of relationships; for his questions are apt to take the form of "Can a man marry his deceased wife's sister?" or what not. Such generalities do not enter at all into the highly concrete scheme of viewing the customs of his tribe imposed on the savage alike by his manner of life and by the very forms of his speech. The so-called "genealogical method" initiated by Dr. Rivers, which the scientific explorer now invariably employs, rests mainly on the use of a concrete type of procedure corresponding to the mental habits of the simple folk under investigation. John, whom you address here, can tell you exactly whether he may, or may not, marry Mary Anne over there; also he can point out his mother, and tell you her name, and the names of his brothers and sisters. You work round the whole group-it very possibly contains no more than a few hundred members at most-and interrogate them one and all about their relationships to this and that individual whom you name. In course of time you have a scheme which you can treat in your own analytic way to your heart's content;

whilst against your system of reckoning affinity you can set up by way of contrast the native system; which can always be obtained by asking each informant what relationship-terms he would apply to the different members of his pedigree, and, reciprocally, what terms they would each apply to him.

Before closing this altogether inadequate sketch of a vast and intricate subject, I would say just one word about the expression of ideas of number. It is quite a mistake to suppose that savages have no sense of number, because the simple-minded European traveller, compiling a short vocabulary in the usual way, can get no equivalent for our numerals, say from 5 to 10. The fact is that the numerical interest has taken a different turn, incorporating itself with other interests of a more concrete kind in linguistic forms to which our own type of language affords no key at all. Thus in the island of Kiwai, at the mouth of the Fly River in New Guinea, the Cambridge Expedition found a whole set of phrases in vogue, whereby the number of subjects acting on the number of objects at a given moment could be concretely specified. To indicate the action of two on many in the past, they said 'rudo', in the present 'durudo'; of many on many in the past 'rumo', in the present 'durumo'; of two on two in the past, 'amarudo', in the present 'amadurudo'; of many on two in the past 'amarumo'; of many on three in the past 'ibidurumo', of many on three in the present 'ibidurudo'; of three on two in the present, 'amabidurumo', of three on two in the past, 'amabirumo', and so on. Meanwhile, words to serve the purpose of pure counting are all the scarcer because hands and feet supply in themselves an excellent means not only of calculating, but likewise of communicating, a number. It is the one case in which gesture-language can claim something like an independent status by the side of speech.

For the rest, it does not follow that the mind fails to appreciate numerical relations, because the tongue halts in the matter of symbolizing them abstractly. A certain high official, when presiding over the Indian census, was informed by a subordinate that it was impossible to elicit from a certain jungle tribe any account of the number of their huts, for the simple and sufficient reason that they could not count above three. The director, who happened to be a man of keen anthropological insight, had therefore himself to come to the rescue. Assembling the tribal elders, he placed a stone on the ground, saying to one "This is your hut," and to another "This is your hut," as he placed a second stone a little way from the first. "And now where is yours?" he asked a third. The natives at once entered into the spirit of the game, and in a short time there was plotted out a plan of the whole settlement, which subsequent verification proved to be both geographically and numerically correct and complete. This story may serve to show how nature supplies man with a ready reckoner in his faculty of perception, which suffices well enough for the affairs of the simpler sort of life. One knows how a shepherd can take in the numbers of a flock at a glance. For the higher flights of experience, however, especially when the unseen and merely possible has to be dealt with, percepts must give way to concepts; massive consciousness must give way to thinking by means of representations pieced together out of elements rendered distinct by previous dissection of the total impression; in short, a concrete must give way to an analytic way of grasping the meaning of things. Moreover, since thinking is little more or less than, as Plato put it, a silent conversation with oneself, to possess an analytic language is to be more than half-way on the road to the analytic mode of intelligence-the mode of thinking by distinct concepts.

If there is a moral to this chapter, it must be that, whereas it is the duty of the civilized overlords of primitive folk to leave them their old institutions so far as they are not directly prejudicial to their gradual advancement in culture, since to lose touch with one's home-world is for the savage to lose heart altogether and die; yet this consideration hardly applies at all to the native language. If the tongue of an advanced people can be substituted, it is for the good of all concerned. It is rather the fashion now-a-days amongst anthropologists to lay it down as an axiom that the typical savage and the typical peasant of Europe stand exactly on a par in respect to their power of general intelligence.

SOCIAL ORGANIZATION

If an explorer visits a savage tribe with intent to get at the true meaning of their life, his first duty, as every anthropologist will tell him, is to acquaint himself thoroughly with the social organization in all its forms. The reason for this is simply that only by studying the outsides of other people can we hope to arrive at what is going on inside them. "Institutions" will be found a convenient word to express all the externals of the life of man in society, so far as they reflect intelligence and purpose. Similarly, the internal or subjective states thereto corresponding may be collectively described as "beliefs." Thus, the field-worker's cardinal maxim can be phrased as follows: Work up to the beliefs by way of the institutions.

Further, there are two ways in which a given set of institutions can be investigated, and of these one, so far as it is practicable, should precede the other. First, the institutions should be examined as so many wheels in a social machine that is taken as if it were standing still. You simply note the characteristic make of each, and how it is placed in relation to the rest. Regarded in this static way, the institutions appear as "forms of social organization." Afterwards, the machine is supposed to be set going, and you contemplate the parts in movement. Regarded thus dynamically, the institutions appear as "customs."

In this chapter, then, something will be said about the forms of social organization prevailing amongst peoples of the lower culture. Our interest will be confined to the social morphology. In subsequent chapters we shall go on to what might be called, by way of contrast, the physiology of social life. In other words, we shall briefly consider the legal and religious customs, together with the associated beliefs.

How do the forms of social organization come into being? Does some one invent them? Does the very notion of organization imply an organizer? Or, like Topsy, do they simply grow? Are they natural crystallizations that take place when people are thrown together? So long as we are pursuing anthropology and not philosophy-in other words, are piecing together events historically according as they appear to follow one another, and are not discussing the ultimate question of the relation of mind to matter, and which of the two in the long run governs which-we must be prepared to recognize both physical necessity and spiritual freedom as interpenetrating factors in human life. In the meantime, when considering the subject of social organization, we shall do well to keep asking ourselves all along, how far does force of circumstances, and how far does the force of intelligent purpose, account for such and such a net result?

It is well known how the invention of machinery in the middle of the eighteenth century brought about that industrial revolution, the social and political effects of which are still developing at this hour. Well, I venture to put it forward as a proposition which applies to human evolution, so far back as our evidence goes, that history is the history of great inventions. Of course, it is true that climate and geographical conditions in general help to determine the nature and quantity of the food-supply; so that, for instance, however much versed you may be in the art of agriculture, you cannot get corn to grow on the shores of the Arctic sea. But, given the needful inventions, superior weapons for instance, you need never allow yourselves to be shoved away into such an inhospitable region; to which you presumably do not retire voluntarily, unless, indeed, the state of your arts-for instance, your skill in hunting or taming the reindeer-inclines you to make a paradise of the tundra.

Suppose it granted, then, that a given people's arts and inventions, whether directly or indirectly productive, are capable of a certain average yield of food, it is certain, as Malthus and Darwin would remind us, that human fertility can be reckoned on to bring the numbers up to a limit bearing a more or less constant ratio to the means of subsistence.

At length we reach our more immediate subject-namely, social organization. In what sense, if any, is social organization dependent on numbers? Unfortunately, it is too large a question to thrash out here. I may, however, refer the reader to the ingenious classification of the peoples of the world, by reference to the degree of their social organization and culture, which is attempted by Mr. Sutherland in his 'Origin and Growth of the Moral Instinct'. He there tries to show that a certain size of population can be correlated with each grade in the scale of human evolution-at any rate up to the point at which full-blown civilization is reached, when cases like that of Athens under Pericles, or Florence under the Medici, would probably cause him some trouble. For instance, he makes out that the lowest savages, Veddas, Pygmies, and so on, form groups of from ten to forty; whereas those who are but one degree less backward, such as the Australian natives, average from fifty to two hundred; whilst most of the North American tribes, who represent the next stage of general advance, run from a hundred up to five hundred. At this point he takes leave of the peoples he would class as "savage," their leading characteristic from the economic point of view being that they lead the more or less wandering life of hunters or of mere "gatherers." He then goes on to arrange similarly, in an ascending series of three divisions, the peoples that he terms "barbarian." Economically they are either sedentary, with a more or less developed agriculture, or, if nomad, pursue the pastoral mode of life. His lowest type of group, which includes the Iroquois, Maoris, and so forth, ranges from one thousand to five thousand; next come loosely organized states, such as Dahomey or Ashanti, where the numbers may reach one hundred thousand; whilst he makes barbarism culminate in more firmly compacted communities, such as are to be found, for example, in Abyssinia or Madagascar, the population of which he places at about half a million.

Besides food, however, there is a second elemental condition which vitally affects the human race; and that is sex. Social organization thus comes to have a twofold aspect. On the one hand, and perhaps primarily, it is an organization of the food-quest. On the other hand, hardly less fundamentally, it is an organization of marriage. In what follows, the two aspects will be considered more or less together, as to a large extent they overlap. Primitive men, like other social animals, hang together naturally in the hunting pack, and no less naturally in the family; and at a very rudimentary stage of evolution there probably is very little distinction between the two. When, however, for some reason or other which anthropologists have still to discover, man takes to the institution of exogamy, the law of marrying-out, which forces men and women to unite who are members of more or less distinct food-groups, then, as we shall presently see, the matrimonial aspect of social organization tends to overshadow the politico-economic; if only because the latter can usually take care of itself, whereas to marry a perfect stranger is an embarrassing operation that might be expected to require a certain amount of arrangement on both sides.

To illustrate the pre-exogamic stage of human society is not so easy as it may seem; for, though it is possible to find examples, especially amongst Negritos such as the Andamanese or Bushmen, of peoples of the rudest culture, and living in very small communities, who apparently know neither exogamy nor what so often accompanies it, namely, totemism, we can never be certain whether we are dealing in such a case with the genuinely primitive, or merely with the degenerate. For instance, the chapter on the forms of social organization in Professor Hobhouse's 'Morals in Evolutionstarts off with an account of the system in vogue amongst the Veddas of the Ceylon jungle, his description being founded on the excellent observations of the brothers Sarasin. Now it is perfectly true that some of the Veddas appear to afford a perfect instance of what is sometimes called "the natural family." A tract of a few miles square forms the beat of a small group of families, four or five at most, which, for the most part, singly or in pairs, wander round hunting, fishing, gathering honey and digging up the wild yams; whilst they likewise take shelter together in shallow caves, where a roof, a piece of skin to lie on-though this is not essential-and, that most precious luxury of all, a fire, represent, apart from food, the sum total of their creature comforts.

Now, under these circumstances, it is not, perhaps, wonderful that the relationships within a group should be decidedly close. Indeed, the correct thing is for the children of a brother and sister to marry; though not, it would seem, for the children of two brothers or of two sisters. And yet there is no approach to promiscuity, but, on the contrary, a very strict monogamy, infidelities being as rare as they are deeply resented. That they had clans of some sort was, indeed, known to Professor Hobhouse and to the authorities whom he follows; but these clans are dismissed as having but the slightest organization and very few functions. An entirely new light, however, has been thrown on the meaning of this clan-system by the recent researches of Dr. and Mrs. Seligmann. It now turns out that some of the Veddas are exogamous-that is to say, are obliged by custom to marry outside their own clan-though others are not. The question then arises, Which, for the Veddas, is the older system, marrying-out or marrying-in? Seeing what a miserable remnant the Veddas are cannot but believe that we have here the case of a formerly exogamous people, groups of which have been forced to marry-in, simply because the alternative was not to marry at all. Of course, it is possible to argue that in so doing they merely reverted to what was once everywhere the primeval condition of man. But at this point historical science tails off into mere guesswork.

We reach relatively firm ground, on the other hand, when we pass on to consider the social organization of such exogamous and totemic peoples as the natives of Australia. The only trouble here is that the subject is too vast and complicated to permit of a handling at once summary and simple. Perhaps the most useful thing that can be done for the reader in a short space is to provide him with a few elementary distinctions, applying not only to the Australians, but more or less to totemic societies in general. With the help of these he may proceed to grapple for himself with the mass of highly interesting but bewildering details concerning social organization to be found in any of the leading first-hand authorities. For instance, for Australia he can do no better than consult the two fascinating works of Messrs. Spencer and Gillen on the Central tribes, or the no less illuminating volume of Howitt on the natives of the South-eastern region; whilst for North America there are many excellent monographs to choose from amongst those issued by the Bureau of Ethnology of the Smithsonian Institution. Or, if he is content to allow some one else to collect the material for him, his best plan will be to consult Dr. Frazer's monumental treatise, 'Totemism and Exogamy', which epitomizes the known facts for the whole wide world, as surveyed region by region.

The first thing to grasp is that, for peoples of this type, social organization is, primarily and on the face of it, identical with kinship-organization. Before proceeding further, let us see what kinship means. Distinguish kinship from consanguinity. Consanguinity is a physical fact. It depends on birth, and covers all one's real blood-relationships, whether recognized by society or not. Kinship, on the other hand, is a sociological fact. It depends on the conventional system of counting descent. Thus it may exclude real relationships; whilst, contrariwise, it may include such as are purely fictitious, as when some one is allowed by law to adopt a child as if it were his own. Now, under civilized conditions, though there is, as we have just seen, such an institution as adoption, whilst, again, there is the case of the illegitimate child, who can claim consanguinity, but can never, in English law at least, attain to kinship, yet, on the whole, we are hardly conscious of the difference between the genuine blood-tie and the social institution that is modelled more or less closely upon it. In primitive society, however, consanguinity tends to be wider than kinship by as much again. In other words, in the recognition of kinship one entire side of the family is usually left clean out of account. A man's kin comprises either his mother's people or his father's people, but not both. Remember that by the law of exogamy, the father and mother are strangers to each other. Hence, primitive society, as it were, issues a judgment of Solomon to the effect that, since they are not prepared to halve their child, it must belong body and soul either to one party or to the other.

We may now go on to analyse this one-sided type of kinship-organization a little more fully. There are three elementary principles that combine to produce it. They are exogamy, lineage and totemism. A word must be said about each in turn.

Exogamy presents no difficulty until you try to account for its origin. It simply means marrying-out, in contrast to endogamy, or marrying-in. Suppose there were a village composed entirely of McIntyres and McIntoshes, and suppose that fashion compelled every McIntyre to marry a McIntosh, and every McIntosh a McIntyre, whilst to marry an outsider, say a McBean, was bad form for McIntyres and McIntoshes alike; then the two clans would be exogamous in respect to each other, whereas the village as a whole would be endogamous.

Lineage is the principle of reckoning descent along one or other of two lines-namely, the mother's line or the father's. The former method is termed matrilineal, the latter patrilineal. It sometimes, but by no means invariably, happens, when descent is counted matrilineally, that the wife stays with her people, and the husband has the status of a mere visitor and alien. In such a case the marriage is called matrilocal; otherwise it is patrilocal. Again, when the matrilocal type of marriage prevails, as likewise often when it does not, the wife and her people, rather than the father and his people, exercise supreme authority over the children. This is known as the matripotestal, as contrasted with the patripotestal, type of family. When the matrilineal, matrilocal and matripotestal conditions are found together, we have mother-right at its fullest and strongest. Where we get only two out of the three, or merely the first by itself, most authorities would still speak of mother-right; though it may be questioned how far the word mother-right, or the corresponding, now almost discarded, expression, "the matriarchate," can be safely used without further explanation, since it tends to imply a right (in the legal sense) and an authority, which in these circumstances is often no more than nominal.

Totemism, in the specific form that has to do with kinship, means that a social group depends for its identity on a certain intimate and exclusive relation in which it stands towards an animal-kind, or a plant-kind, or, more rarely, a class of inanimate objects, or, very rarely, something that is individual and not a kind or class at all. Such a totem, in the first place, normally provides the social group with its name. (The Boy Scouts, who call themselves Foxes, Peewits, and so on, according to their different patrols, have thus reverted to a very ancient usage.) In the second place, this name tends to be the outward and visible sign of an inward and spiritual grace that, somehow flowing from the totem to the totemites, sanctifies their communion. They are "all-one-flesh" with one another, as certain of the Australians phrase it, because they are "all-one-flesh" with the totem. Or, again, a man whose totem was 'ngaui', the sun, said that his name was 'ngauiand he "was" 'ngaui'; though he was equally ready to put it in another way, explaining that 'ngaui"owned" him. If we wish to express the matter comprehensively, and at the same time to avoid language suggestive of a more advanced mysticism, we may perhaps describe the totem as, from this point of view, the totemite's "luck."

There is considerable variation, however, to be found in the practices and beliefs of a more or less religious kind that are associated with this form of totemism; though almost always there are some. Sometimes the totem is thought of as an ancestor, or as the common fund of life out of which the totemites are born and into which they go back when they die. Sometimes the totem is held to be a very present help in time of trouble, as when a kangaroo, by hopping along in a special way, warns the kangaroo-man of impending danger. Sometimes, on the other hand, the kangaroo-man thinks of himself mainly as the helper of the kangaroo, holding ceremonies in order that the kangaroos may wax fat and multiply. Again, almost invariably the totemite shows some respect towards his totem, refraining, for instance, from slaying and eating the totem-animal, unless it be in some specially solemn and sacramental way.

The upshot of these considerations is that if the totem is, on the face of it, a name, the savage answers the question, "What's in a name?" by finding in the name that makes him one with his brethren a wealth of mystic meaning, such as deepens for him the feeling of social solidarity to an extent that it takes a great effort on our part to appreciate.

Having separately examined the three principles of exogamy, lineage and totemism, we must now try to see how they work together. Generalization in regard to these matters is extremely risky, not to say rash; nevertheless, the following broad statements may serve the reader as working hypotheses, that he can go on to test for himself by looking into the facts. Firstly, exogamy and totemism, whether they be in origin distinct or not, tend in practice to go pretty closely together. Secondly, lineage, or the one-sided system of reckoning descent, is more or less independent of the other two principles.

If, instead of consulting the evidence that is to hand about the savage world as it exists to-day, you read some book crammed full with theories about social origins, you probably come away with the impression that totemic society is entirely an affair of clans. Some such notion as the following is precipitated in your mind. You figure to yourself two small food-groups, whose respective beats are, let us say, on each side of a river. For some unknown reason they are totemic, one group calling itself Cockatoo, the other calling itself Crow, whilst each feels in consequence that its members are "all-one-flesh" in some mysterious and moving sense. Again, for some unknown reason each is exogamous, so that matrimonial alliances are bound to take place across the river. Lastly, each has mother-right of the full-blown kind. The Cockatoo-girls and the Crow-girls abide each on their own side of the river, where they are visited by partners from across the water; who, whether they tend to stay and make themselves useful, or are merely intermittent in their attentions, remain outsiders from the totemic point of view and are treated as such. The children, meanwhile, grow up in the Cockatoo and Crow quarters respectively as little Cockatoos or Crows. If they need to be chastised, a Cockatoo hand, not necessarily the mother's, but perhaps her brother's-never the father's, however-administers the slap. When they grow up, they take their chances for better and worse with the mother's people; fighting when they fight, though it be against the father's people; sharing in the toils and the spoils of the chase; inheriting the weapons and any other property that is handed on from one generation to another; and, last but not least, taking part in the totemic mysteries that disclose to the elect the inner meaning of being a Cockatoo or a Crow, as the case may be.

Now such a picture of the original clan and of the original inter-clan organization is very pretty and easy to keep in one's head. And when one is simply guessing about the first beginnings of things, there is something to be said for starting from some highly abstract and simple concept, which is afterwards elaborated by additions and qualifications until the developed notion comes near to matching the complexity of the real facts. Such speculations, then, are quite permissible and even necessary in their place. To do justice, however, to the facts about totemic society, as known to us by actual observation, it remains to note that the clan is by no means the only form of social organization that it displays.

The clan, it is true, whether matrilineal or patrilineal, tends at the totemic level of society to eclipse the family. The natural family, of course-that is to say, the more or less permanent association of father, mother and children, is always there in some shape and to some extent. But, so long as the one-sided method of counting descent prevails, and is reinforced by totemism, the family cannot attain to the dignity of a formally recognized institution. On the other hand, the totemic clan, of all the formally recognized groupings of society to which an individual belongs in virtue of his birth and kinship, is, so to speak, the most specific. As the Australian puts it, it makes him what he "is." His social essence is to be a Cockatoo or a Crow. Consequently his first duty is towards his clan and its members, human and not-human. Wherever there are clans, and so long as there is any totemism worthy of the name, this would seem to be the general law.

Besides the specific unity, however, provided by the clan, there are wider, and, as it were, more generic unities into which a man is born, in totemic society of the complex type that is found in the actual world of to-day.

First, he belongs to a phratry. In Australia the tribe-a term to be defined presently-is nearly always split up into two exogamous divisions, which it is usual to call phratries. Then, in some of the Australian tribes, the phratry is subdivided into two, and, in others, into four portions, between which exogamy takes place according to a curious criss-cross scheme. These exogamous subdivisions, which are peculiar to Australia, are known as matrimonial classes. Dr. Frazer thinks that they are the result of deliberate arrangement on the part of native statesmen; and certainly he is right in his contention that there is an artificial and man-made look about them. The system of phratries, on the other hand, whether it carves up the tribe into two, or, as sometimes in North America and elsewhere, into more than two primary divisions, under which the clans tend to group themselves in a more or less orderly way, has all the appearance of a natural development out of the clan-system. Thus, to revert to the imaginary case of the Cockatoos and Crows practising exogamy across the river, it seems easy to understand how the numbers on both sides might increase until, whilst remaining Cockatoos and Crows for cross-river purposes, they would find it necessary to adopt among themselves subordinate distinctions; such as would be sure to model themselves on the old Cockatoo-Crow principle of separate totemic badges. But we must not wander off into questions of origin. It is enough for our present purpose to have noted the fact that, within the tribe, there are normally other forms of social grouping into which a man is born, as well as the clan.

Now we come to the tribe. This may be described as the political unit. Its constitution tends to be lax and its functions vague. One way of seizing its nature is to think of it as the social union within which exogamy takes place. The intermarrying groups naturally hang together, and are thus in their entirety endogamous, in the sense that marriage with pure outsiders is disallowed by custom. Moreover, by mingling in this way, they are likely to attain to the use of a common dialect, and a common name, speaking of themselves, for instance, as "the men," and lumping the rest of humanity together as "foreigners." To act together, however, as, for instance, in war, in order to repel incursions on the part of the said foreigners, is not easy without some definite organization. In Australia, where there is very little war, this organization is mostly wanting. In North America, on the other hand, amongst the more advanced and warlike tribes, we find regular tribal officers, and some approach to a political constitution. Yet in Australia there is at least one occasion when a sort of tribal gathering takes place-namely, when their elaborate ceremonies for the initiation of the youths is being held.

It would seem, however, that these ceremonies are, as often as not, intertribal rather than tribal. So similar are the customs and beliefs over wide areas, that groups with apparently little or nothing else in common will assemble together, and take part in proceedings that are something like a Pan-Anglican Congress and a World's Fair rolled into one. To this indefinite type of intertribal association the term "nation" is sometimes applied. Only when there is definite organization, as never in Australia, and only occasionally in North America, as amongst the Iroquois, can we venture to describe it as a genuine "confederacy."

No doubt the reader's head is already in a whirl, though perpetrated endless sins of omission and of commission as well, in order to simplify the glorious confusion of the subject of the social organization prevailing in what is conveniently but loosely lumped together as totemic society. Thus, have omitted to mention that sometimes the totems seem to have nothing to do at all with the social organization; as, for example, amongst the famous Arunta of central Australia, whom Messrs. Spencer and Gillen have so carefully described and again, refrained from pointing out that sometimes there are exogamous divisions-some would call them moieties to distinguish them from phratries-which have no clans grouped under them, and, on the other hand, have themselves little or no resemblance to totemic clans. These, and ever so many other exceptional cases.

An even more serious kind of omission is the following. The social organization with the kinship organization-namely, that into which a man is born in consequence of the marriage laws and the system of reckoning descent. But there are other secondary features of what can only be classed as social organization, which have nothing to do with kinship. Sex, for instance, has a direct bearing on social status. The men and the women often form markedly distinct groups; so that we are almost reminded of the way in which the male and the female linnets go about in separate flocks as soon as the pairing season is over. Of course, disparity of occupation has something to do with it. But, for the native mind, the difference evidently goes far deeper than that. In some parts of Australia there are actually sex-totems, signifying that each sex is all-one-flesh, a mystic corporation. And, all the savage world over, there is a feeling that woman is uncanny, a thing apart, which feeling is probably responsible for most of the special disabilities-and the special privileges-that are the lot of woman at the present day.

Again, age likewise has considerable influence on social status. It is not merely a case of being graded as a youth until once for all you legally "come of age," and are enrolled, amongst the men. The grading of ages is frequently most elaborate, and each batch mounts the social ladder step by step. Just as, at the university, each year has apportioned to it by public opinion the things it may do and the things it may not do, whilst, later on, the bachelor, the master, and the doctor stand each a degree higher in respect of academic rank; so in darkest Australia, from youth up to middle age at least, a man will normally undergo a progressive initiation into the secrets of life, accompanied by a steady widening in the sphere of his social duties and rights.

Lastly, locality affects status, and increasingly as the wandering life gives way to stable occupation. Amongst a few hundred people who are never out of touch with each other, the forms of natal association hold their own against any that local association is likely to suggest in their place. According to natal grouping, therefore, in the broad sense that includes sex and age no less than kinship, the members of the tribe camp, fight, perform magical ceremonies, play games, are initiated, are married, and are buried. But let the tribe increase in numbers, and spread through a considerable area, over the face of which communications are difficult and proportionately rare. Instantly the local group tends to become all in all. Authority and initiative must always rest with the men on the spot; and the old natal combinations, weakened by inevitable absenteeism, at last cease to represent the true framework of the social order. They tend to linger on, of course, in the shape of subordinate institutions. For instance, the totemic groups cease to have direct connection with the marriage system, and, on the strength of the ceremonies associated with them, develop into what are known as secret societies.

Or, again, the clan is gradually overshadowed by the family, so that kinship, with its rights and duties, becomes practically limited to the nearer blood-relations; who, moreover, begin to be treated for practical purposes as kinsmen, even when they are on the side of the family which lineage does not officially recognize. Thus the forms of natal association no longer constitute the backbone of the body politic. Their public importance has gone. Henceforward, the social unit is the local group. The territorial principle comes more and more to determine affinities and functions. Kinship has dethroned itself by its very success. Thanks to the organizing power of kinship, primitive society has grown, and by growing has stretched the birth-tie until it snaps. Some relationships become distant in a local and territorial sense, and thereupon they cease to count. My duty towards my kin passes into my duty towards my neighbour.

Reasons of space make it impossible to survey the further developments to which social organization is subject under the sway of locality. It is, perhaps, less essential to insist on them here, because, whereas totemic society is a thing which we civilized folk have the very greatest difficulty in understanding, we all have direct insight into the meaning of a territorial arrangement; since, from the village community up to the modern state, the same fundamental type of social structure obtains throughout.

Besides local contiguity, however, there is a second principle which greatly helps to shape the social order, as soon as society is sufficiently advanced in its arts and industries to have taken firm root, so to speak, on the earth's surface. This is the principle of private property, and especially of private property in land. The most fundamental of class distinctions is that between rich and poor. That between free and slave, in communities that have slavery, is not at first sight strictly parallel, since there may be a class of poor freemen intermediate between the nobles and the slaves; but it is obvious that in this case, too, private property is really responsible for the mode of grading. Or sometimes social position may seem to depend primarily on industrial occupation, the Indian caste-system providing an instance in point. Since, however, the most honourable occupations in the long run coincide with those that pay best, we come back once again to private property as the ultimate source of social rank, under an economic system of the more developed kind.

In this brief sketch it has been impossible to do more than hint how social organization is relative to numbers, which in their turn are relative to the skill with which the food-quest is carried on. But if, up to a certain point, it be true that the structure of society depends on its mass in a more or less physical way, there is to be borne in mind another aspect of the matter, which also has been hinted at as we went rapidly along. A good deal of intelligence has throughout helped towards the establishing of the social order. If social organization is in part a natural result of the expansion of the population, it is partly also, in the best sense of the word, an artificial creation of the human mind, which has exerted itself to devise modes of grouping whereby men might be enabled to work together in larger and ever larger wholes.

Regarded, however, in the purely external way which a study of its mere structure involves, society appears as a machine-that is to say, appears as the work of intelligence indeed, but not as itself instinct with intelligence. In what follows we shall set the social machine moving. We shall then have a better chance of obtaining an inner view of the driving power. We shall find that we have to abandon the notion that society is a machine. It is more, even, than an organism. It is a communion of souls-souls that, as so many independent, yet interdependent, manifestations of the life-force, are pressing forward in the search for individuality and freedom.

7

Law

The general plan of this little book being to start from the influences that determine man's destiny in a physical, external, necessary sort of way, and to work up gradually to the spiritual, internal, voluntary factors in human nature-that strange "compound of clay and flame" - it seems advisable to consider law before religion, and religion before morality, whether in its collective or individual aspect, for the following reason. There is more sheer constraint to be discerned in law than in religion, whilst religion, in the historical sense which identifies it with organized cult, is more coercive in its mode of regulating life than the moral reason, which compels by force of persuasion.

To one who lives under civilized conditions the phrase "the strong arm of the law" inevitably suggests the policeman. Apart from policemen, magistrates, and the soldiers who in the last resort must be called out to enforce the decrees of the community, it might appear that law could not exist. And certainly it is hard to admit that what is known as mob-law is any law at all. For historical purposes, however, we must be prepared to use the expression "law" rather widely. We must be ready to say that there is law wherever there is punishment on the part of a human society, whether acting in the mass, or through its representatives. Punishment means the infliction of pain on one who is judged to have broken a social rule. Conversely, then, a law is any social rule to the infringement of which punishment is by usage attached. So long as it is recognized that a man breaks a social rule at the risk of pain, and that it is the business of everybody, or of somebody armed with the common authority, to make that risk a reality for the offender, there is law within the meaning of the term as it exists for anthropology.

Punishment, however, is by its very nature an exceptional measure. It is only because the majority are content to follow a social rule, that law and punishment are possible at all. If, again, every one habitually obeys the social rules, law ceases to exist, because it is unnecessary. Now, one reason why it is hard to find any law in primitive society is because, in a general way of speaking, no one dreams of breaking the social rules.

Custom is king, nay tyrant, in primitive society. When Captain Cook asked the chiefs of Tahiti why they ate apart and alone, they simply replied, "Because it is right." And so it always is with the ruder peoples. "'Tis the custom, and there's an end on't" is their notion of a sufficient reason in politics and ethics alike. Now that way lies a rigid conservatism. In the chapter on morality we shall try to discover its inner springs, its psychological conditions. For the present, we may be content to regard custom from the outside, as the social habit of conserving all traditional practices for their own sake and regardless of consequences. Of course, changes are bound to occur, and do occur. But they are not supposed to occur. In theory, the social rules of primitive society are like "the law of the Medes and Persians which altereth not."

This absolute respect for custom has its good and its bad sides. On the one hand, it supplies the element of discipline; without which any society is bound soon to fall to pieces. We are apt to think of the savage as a freakish creature, all moods-at one moment a friend, at the next moment a fiend. So he might be, if it were not for the social drill imposed by his customs. So he is, if you destroy his customs, and expect him nevertheless to behave as an educated and reasonable being. Given, then, a primitive society in a healthy and uncontaminated condition, its members will invariably be found to be on the average more law-abiding, as judged from the standpoint of their own law, than is the case any civilized state.

But now we come to the bad side of custom. Its conserving influence extends to all traditional practices, however unreasonable or perverted. In that amber any fly is apt to be enclosed. Hence the whimsicalities of savage custom. In 'Primitive CultureDr. Tylor tells a good story about the Dyaks of Borneo. The white man's way of chopping down a tree by notching out V-shaped cuts was not according to Dyak custom. Hence, any Dyak caught imitating the European fashion was punished by a fine. And yet so well aware were they that this method was an improvement on their own that, when they could trust each other not to tell, they would surreptitiously use it. These same Dyaks, it may be added, are, according to Mr. A.R. Wallace, the best of observers, "among the most pleasing of savages." They are good-natured, mild, and by no means bloodthirsty in the ordinary relations of life. Yet they are well known to be addicted to the horrid practice of head-hunting. "It was a custom," Mr. Wallace explains, "and as a custom was observed, but it did not imply any extraordinary barbarism or moral delinquency."

The drawback, then, to a reign of pure custom is this: Meaningless injunctions abound, since the value of a traditional practice does not depend on its consequences, but simply on the fact that it is the practice; and this element of irrationality is enough to perplex, till it utterly confounds, the mind capable of rising above routine and reflecting on the true aims and ends of the social life. How to break through "the cake of custom," as Bagehot has called it, is the hardest lesson that humanity has ever had to learn. Customs have often been broken up by the clashing of different societies; but in that case they merely crystallize again into new shapes. But to break through custom by the sheer force of reflection, and so to make rational progress possible, was the intellectual feat of one people, the ancient Greeks; and it is at least highly doubtful if, without their leadership, a progressive civilization would have existed today.

It may be added in parenthesis that customs may linger on indefinitely, after losing, through one cause or another, their place amongst the vital interests of the community. They are, or at any rate seem, harmless; their function is spent. Hence, whilst perhaps the humbler folk still take them more or less seriously, the leaders of society are not at pains to suppress them. Nor would they always find it easy to do so. Something of the primeval man lurks in us all; and these "survivals," as they are termed by the anthropologist, may often in large part correspond to impulses that are by no means dead in us, but rather sleep; and are hence liable to be reawakened, if the environment happens to supply the appropriate stimulus. Witness the fact that survivals, especially when the whirligig of social change brings the uneducated temporarily to the fore, have a way of blossoming forth into revivals; and the state may in consequence have to undergo something equivalent to an operation for appendicitis. The study of so-called survivals, therefore, is a most important branch of anthropology, which cannot unfortunately in this hasty sketch be given its due. It would seem to coincide with the central interest of what is known as folk-lore. Folk-lore, however, tends to broaden out till it becomes almost indistinguishable from general anthropology. There are at least two reasons for this. Firstly, the survivals of custom amongst advanced nations, such as the ancient Greeks or the modern British, are to be interpreted mainly by comparison with the similar institutions still flourishing amongst ruder peoples. Secondly, all these ruder peoples themselves, without exception, have their survivals too. Their customs fall as it were into two layers. On top is the live part of the fire. Underneath are smouldering ashes, which, though dying out on the whole, are yet liable here and there to rekindle into flame.

So much for custom as something on the face of it distinct from law, inasmuch as it seems to dispense with punishment. It remains to note, however, that brute force lurks behind custom, in the form of what Bagehot has called "the persecuting tendency." Just a boy at school who happens to offend against the unwritten code has his life made a burden by the rest of his mates, so in the primitive community the fear of a rough handling causes "I must not" to wait upon "I dare not." One has only to read Mr. Andrew Lang's instructive story of the fate of "Why Why, the first Radical," to realize how amongst savages - and is it so very different amongst ourselves?-it pays much better to be respectable than to play the moral hero.

After all, even under the sway of custom, casual outbreaks are liable to occur. Some one's passions will prove too much for him, and there will be an accident. What happens then in the primitive society? Let us first consider one of the very unorganized communities at the bottom of the evolutionary scale; as, for example, the little Negritos of the Andaman Islands. Their justice, explains Mr. Man, in his excellent account of these people, is administered by the simple method of allowing the aggrieved party to take the law into his own hands. This he usually does by flinging a burning faggot at the offender, or by discharging an arrow at him, though more frequently near him. Meanwhile all others who may be present are apt to beat a speedy retreat, carrying off as much of their property as their haste will allow, and remaining hid in the jungle until sufficient time has elapsed for the quarrel to have blown over. Sometimes, however, friends interpose, and seek to deprive the disputants of their weapons. Should, however, one of them kill the other, nothing is necessarily said or done to him by the rest. Yet conscience makes cowards of us all; so that the murderer, from prudential motives, will not uncommonly absent himself until he judges that the indignation of the victim's friends has sufficiently abated.

Now here we seem to find want of social structure and want of law going together as cause and effect. The "friends" of whom we hear need to be organized into a police force. If we now turn to totemic society, with its elaborate clan-system, it is quite another story. Blood-revenge ranks amongst the foremost of the clansman's social obligations. Over the whole world it stands out by itself as the type of all that law means for the savage. Within the clan, indeed, the maxim of blood for blood does not hold; though there may be another kind of punitive law put into force by the totemites against an erring brother, as, for instance, if they slay one of their number for disregarding the exogamic rule and consorting with a woman who is all-one-flesh with him. But, between clans of the same tribe, the system of blood-revenge requires strict reprisals, according to the principle that some one on the other side, though not necessarily the actual murderer, must die the death. This is known as the principle of collective responsibility; and one of the most interesting problems relating to the evolution of early law is to work out how individual responsibility gradually develops out of collective, until at length, even as each man does, so likewise he suffers.

The collective method of settling one's grievances is natural enough, when men are united into groups bound together by the closest of sentimental ties, and on the other hand there is no central and impartial authority to arbitrate between the parties. One of our crew has been killed by one of your crew. So a stand-up fight takes place. Of course we should like to get at the right man if we could; but, failing that, we are out to kill some one in return, just to teach your crew a lesson. Comparatively early in the day, however, it strikes the savage mind that there are degrees of responsibility. For instance, some one has to call the avenging party together, and to lead it. He will tend to be a real blood-relation, son, father, or brother. Thus he stands out as champion, whilst the rest are in the position of mere seconds. Correspondingly, the other side will tend to thrust forward the actual offender into the office of counter-champion. There is direct evidence to show that, amongst Australians, Eskimo, and so on, whole groups at one time met in battle, but later on were represented by chosen individuals, in the persons of those who were principals in the affair. Thus we arrive at the duel. The transition is seen in such a custom as that of the Port Lincoln black-fellows. The brother of the murdered man must engage the murderer; but any one on either side who might care to join in the fray was at liberty to do so. Hence it is but a step to the formal duel, as found, for instance, amongst the Apaches of North America.

Now the legal duel is an advance on the collective bear-fight, if only because it brings home to the individual perpetrator of the crime that he will have to answer for it. Cranz, the great authority on the Eskimo of Greenland, naively remarks that a Greenlander dare not murder or otherwise wrong another, since it might possibly cost him the life of his best friend. Did the Greenlander know that it would probably cost him his own life, his sense of responsibility, we may surmise, might be somewhat quickened. On the other hand, duelling is not a satisfactory way of redressing the balance, since it merely gives the powerful bully an opportunity of adding a second murder to the first. Hence the ordeal marks an advance in legal evolution. A good many Australian peoples, for example, have reached the stage of requiring the murderer to submit to a shower of spears or boomerangs at the hands of the aggrieved group, on the mutual understanding that the blood-revenge ends here.

Luckily, however, for the murderer, it often takes time to bring him to book; and angry passions are apt in the meanwhile to subside. The ruder savages are not so bloodthirsty as we are apt to imagine. War has evolved like everything else; and with it has evolved the man who likes fighting for its own sake. So, in place of a life for a life, compensation-"pacation," as it is technically termed-comes to be recognized as a reasonable 'quid pro quo'. Constantly we find custom at the half-way stage. If the murderer is caught soon, he is killed; but if he can stave off the day of justice, he escapes with a fine. When private property has developed, the system of blood-fines becomes most elaborate. Amongst the Iroquois the manslayer must redeem himself from death by means of no less than sixty presents to the injured kin; one to draw the axe out of the wound, a second to wipe the blood away, a third to restore peace to the land, and so forth. According to the collective principle, the clansmen on one side share the price of atonement, and on the other side must tax themselves in order to make it up. Shares are on a scale proportionate to degrees of relationship. Or, again, further nice calculations are required, if it is sought to adjust the gross amount of the payment to the degree of guilt. Hence it is not surprising that, when a more or less barbarous people, such as the Anglo-Saxons, came to require a written law, it should be almost entirely taken up by regulations about blood-fines, that had become too complicated for the people any longer to keep in their heads.

So far we have been considering the law of blood-revenge as purely an affair between the clans concerned; the rest of the tribal public keeping aloof, very much in the style of the Andamanese bystanders who retire into the jungle when there is a prospect of a row. But with the development of a central authority, whether in the shape of the rule of many or of one, the public control of the blood-feud begins to assert itself; for the good reason that endless vendetta is a dissolving force, which the larger and more stable type of society cannot afford to tolerate if it is to survive. The following are a few instances illustrative of the transition from private to public jurisdiction. In North America, Africa, and elsewhere, we find the chief or chiefs pronouncing sentence, but the clan or family left to carry it out as best they can. Again, the kin may be entrusted with the function of punishment, but obliged to carry it out in the way prescribed by the authorities; as, for instance, in Abyssinia, where the nearest relation executes the manslayer in the presence of the king, using exactly the same kind of weapon as that with which the murder was committed. Or the right of the kin to punish dwindles to a mere form. Thus in Afghanistan the elders make a show of handing over the criminal to his accusers, who must, however, comply strictly with the wishes of the assembly; whilst in Samoa the offender was bound and deposited before the family "as if to signify that he lay at their mercy," and the chief saw to the rest. Finally, the state, in the person of its executive officers, both convicts and executes.

When the state is represented by a single ruler, crime tends to become an offence against "the king's peace"-or, in the language of Roman law, against his "majesty." Henceforward, the easy-going system of getting off with a fine is at an end, and murder is punished with the utmost sternness. In such a state as Dahomey, in the old days of independence, there may have been a good deal of barbarity displayed in the administration of justice, but at any rate human life was no less effectively protected by the law than it was, say, in medieval Europe.

The evolution of the punishment of murder affords the typical instance of the development of a legal sanction in primitive society. Other forms, however, of the forcible repression of wrong-doing deserve a more or less passing notice.

Adultery is, even amongst the ruder peoples, a transgression that is reckoned only a degree less grave than manslaughter; especially as manslaughter is a usual consequence of it, quarrels about women constituting one of the chief sources of trouble in the savage world. With a single interesting exception, the stages in the development of the law against adultery are exactly the same as in the case already examined. Whole kins fight about it. Then duelling is substituted. Then duelling gives way to the ordeal. Then, after the penalty has long wavered between death and a fine, fines become the rule, so long as the kins are allowed to settle the matter. If, however, the community comes to take cognizance of the offence, severer measures ensue. The one noticeable difference in the two developments is the following. Whereas murder is an offence against the chief's "majesty," and as such a criminal offence, adultery, like theft, with which primitive law is wont to associate it as an offence against property, tends to remain a purely civil affair. Kafir law, for example, according to Maclean, draws this distinction very clearly.

It remains to add as regards adultery that, so far, we have only been considering the punishment that falls on the guilty man. The guilty woman's fate is a matter relating to a distinct department of primitive law. Family jurisdiction, as we find it, for instance, in an advanced community such as ancient Rome, meant the right of the 'pater familias', the head of the house, to subject his 'familia', or household, which included his wife, his children (up to a certain age), and his slaves, to such domestic discipline as he saw fit. Such family jurisdiction was more or less completely independent of state jurisdiction; and, indeed, has remained so in Europe until comparatively recent times.

What light, then, does the study of primitive society throw on the first beginnings of family law as administered by the house-father? To answer this question at all adequately would involve the writing of many pages on the evolution of the family. For our present purpose, all turns on the distinction between the matripotestal and the patripotestal family. If the man and the woman were left to fight it out alone, the latter, despite the "shrewish sanction" that she possesses in her tongue, must inevitably bow to the principle that might is right. But, as long as marriage is matrilocal-that is to say, allows the wife to remain at home amongst male defenders of her own clan-she can safely lord it over her stranger husband; and there can scarcely be adultery on her part, since she can always obtain divorce by simply saying, Go! Things grow more complicated when the wife lives amongst her husband's people, and, nevertheless, the system of counting descent favours her side of the family and not his. Does the mere fact that descent is matrilineal tend to imply on the whole that the mother's kin take a more active interest in her, and are more effective in protecting her from hurt, whether undeserved or deserved? It is no easy problem to settle. Dr. Steinmetz, however, in his important work on 'The Evolution of Punishment(in German), seeks to show that under mother-right, in all its forms taken together, the adulteress is more likely to escape with a light penalty, or with none at all, than under father-right. Whatever be the value of the statistical method that he employs, at any rate it makes out the death penalty to be inflicted in only a third of his cases under the former system, but in about half under the latter.

We must be content with a mere glance at other types of wrong-doing which, whilst sooner or later recognized by the law of the community, affect its members in their individual capacity. Theft and slander are cases in point.

Amongst the ruder savages there cannot be much stealing, because there is next to nothing to steal. Nevertheless, groups are apt to quarrel over hunting and fishing claims; whilst the division of the spoils of the chase may give rise to disputes, which call for the interposition of leading men. We even occasionally find amongst Australians the formal duel employed to decide cases of the violation of property-rights. Not, however, until the arts of life have advanced, and wealth has created the two classes of "haves" and "have-nots," does theft become an offence of the first magnitude, which the central authority punishes with corresponding severity.

As regards slander, though it might seem a slight matter, it must be remembered that the savage cannot stand up for a moment again an adverse public opinion; so that to rob him of his good name is to take away all that makes life worth living. To shout out, Long-nose! Sunken-eyes! or Skin-and-bone! usually leads to a fight in Andamanese circles, as

Mr. Man informs us. Nor, again, is it conducive to peace in Australian society to sing as follows about the staying-powers of a fellow-tribesman temporarily overtaken by European liquor: "Spirit like emu-as a whirlwind-pursues-lays violent hold on travelling-uncle of mine (this being particularly derisive) - tired out with fatigue-throws himself down helpless." Amongst more advanced peoples, therefore, slander and abuse are sternly checked. They constitute a ground for a civil action in Kafir law; whilst we even hear of an African tribe, the Ba-Ngindo, who rejoice in the special institution of a peace-maker, whose business is to compose troubles arising from this vexatious source.

Let us now turn to another class of offences, such as, from the first, are regarded as so prejudicial to the public interest that the community as a whole must forcibly put them down.

Cases of what may be termed military discipline fall under this head. Even when the functions of the commander are undeveloped, and war is still "an affair of armed mobs," shirking-a form of crime which, to do justice to primitive society, is rare-is promptly and effectively resented by the host. Amongst American tribes the coward's arms are taken away from him; he is made to eat with the dogs; or perhaps a shower of arrows causes him to "run the gauntlet." The traitor, on the other hand, is inevitably slain without mercy-tied to a tree and shot, or, it may be, literally hacked to pieces. Naturally, with the evolution of war, these spontaneous outbursts of wrath and disgust give way to a more formal system of penalties. To trace out this development fully, however, would entail a lengthy disquisition on the growth of kingship in one of its most important aspects. If constant fighting turns the tribe into something like a standing army, the position of war-lord, as, for instance, amongst the Zulus, is bound to become both permanent and of all-embracing authority. There is, however, another side to the history of kingship, as the following considerations will help to make clear.

Public safety is construed by the ruder type of man not so much in terms of freedom from physical danger-unless such a danger, the onset of another tribe, for instance, is actually imminent-as in terms of freedom from spiritual, or mystic, danger. The fear of ill-luck, in other words, is the bogy that haunts him night and day. Hence his life is enmeshed, as Dr. Frazer puts it, in a network of taboos. A taboo is anything that one must not do lest ill-luck befall. And ill-luck is catching, like an infectious disease. If my next-door neighbour breaks a taboo, and brings down a visitation on himself, depend upon it some of its unpleasant consequences will be passed on to me and mine. Hence, if some one has committed an act that is not merely a crime but a sin, it is every one's concern to wipe out that sin; which is usually done by wiping out the sinner. Mobbish feeling always inclines to violence. In the mob, as a French psychologist has said, ideas neutralize each other, but emotions aggrandize each other. Now war-feeling is a mobbish experience that, I daresay, some of my readers have tasted; and we have seen how it leads the unorganized levy of a savage tribe to make short work of the coward and traitor. But war-fever is a mild variety of mobbish experience as compared with panic in any form, and with superstitious panic most of all. Being attacked in the dark, as it were, causes the strongest to lose their heads.

Hence it is not hard to understand how it comes about that the violator of a taboo is the central object of communal vengeance in primitive society. The most striking instance of such a taboo-breaker is the man or woman who disregards the prohibition against marriage within the kin-in other words, violates the law of exogamy. To be thus guilty of incest is to incite in the community at large a horror which, venting itself in what Bagehot calls a "wild spasm of wild justice," involves certain death for the offender. To interfere with a grave, to pry into forbidden mysteries, to eat forbidden meats, and so on, are further examples of transgressions liable to be thus punished.

Falling under the same general category of sin, though distinct from the violation of taboo, is witchcraft. This consists in trafficking, or at any rate in being supposed to traffic, with powers of evil for sinister and anti-social ends. We have only to remember how England, in the seventeenth century, could work itself up into a frenzy on this account to realize how, in an African society even of the better sort, the "smelling-out" and destroying of a witch may easily become a general panacea for quieting the public nerves.

When crimes and sins, affairs of state and affairs of church thus overlap and commingle in primitive jurisprudence, it is no wonder if the functions of those who administer the law should tend to display a similar fusion of aspects. The chief, or king, has a "divine right," and is himself in one or another sense divine, even whilst he takes the lead in regard to all such matters as are primarily secular. The earliest written codes, such as the Mosaic Books of the Law, with their strange medley of injunctions concerning things profane and sacred, accurately reflect the politico-religious character of all primitive authority.

Indeed, it is only by an effort of abstraction that the present chapter has been confined to the subject of law, as distinguished from the subject of the following chapter, namely, religion. Any crime, as notably murder, and even under certain circumstances theft, is apt to be viewed by the ruder peoples either as a violation of taboo, or as some closely related form of sin. Nay, within the limits of the clan, legal punishment can scarcely be said to be in theory possible; the sacredness of the blood-tie lending to any chastisement that may be inflicted on an erring kinsman the purely religious complexion of a sacrifice, an act of excommunication, a penance, or what not. Thus almost insensibly we are led on to the subject of religion from the study of the legal sanction; this very term "sanction," which is derived from Roman law, pointing in the same direction, since it originally stood for the curse which was appended in order to secure the inviolability of a legal enactment.

8

Religion and Morality

Magic and religion, according to the view belong to the same department of human experience-one of the two great departments, the two worlds, one might almost call them, into which human experience, throughout its whole history, has been divided. Together they belong to the supernormal world, the 'x'-region of experience, the region of mental twilight.

Magic include all bad ways, and religion all good ways, of dealing with the supernormal-bad and good, of course, not as we may happen to judge them, but as the society concerned judges them. Sometimes, indeed, the people themselves hardly know where to draw the line between the two; and, in that case, the anthropologist cannot well do it for them. But every primitive society thinks witchcraft bad. Witchcraft consists in leaguing oneself with supernormal powers of evil in order to effect selfish and anti-social ends. Witchcraft, then, is genuine magic-black magic of the devil's colour. On the other hand, every primitive society also distinguishes certain salutary ways of dealing with supernormal powers. All these ways taken together constitute religion. For the rest, there will always be a mass of more or less evaporated beliefs, going with practices that have more or less lost their hold on the community. These belong to the folklore which every people has. Under this or some closely related head must also be set down the mass of mere wonder-tales, due to the play of fancy, and without direct bearing on the serious pursuits of life.

The world to which neither magic nor religion belongs, but to which physical science, the knowledge of how to deal mechanically with material things, does belong wholly, is the workaday world, the region of normal, commonplace, calculable happenings. With our telescopes and microscopes we see farther and deeper into things than does the savage. Yet the savage has excellent eyes. What he sees he sees. Consequently, we must duly allow for the fact that there is for him, as well as for us, a "natural," that is to say, normal and workaday world; even though it be far narrower in extent than ours. The savage is not perpetually spook-haunted. On the contrary, when he is engaged on the daily round, and all is going well, he is as careless and happy as a child.

But savage life has few safeguards. Crisis is a frequent, if intermittent, element in it. Hunger, sickness and war are examples of crisis. Birth and death are crises. Marriage is usually regarded by humanity as a crisis. So is initiation-the turning-point in one's career, when one steps out into the world of men. Now what, in terms of mind, does crisis mean? It means that one is at one's wits' end; that the ordinary and expected has been replaced by the extraordinary and unexpected; that we are projected into the world of the unknown. And in that world of the unknown we must miserably abide until, somehow, confidence is restored.

Psychologically regarded, then, the function of religion is to restore men's confidence when it is shaken by crisis. Men do not seek crisis; they would always run away from it, if they could. Crisis seeks them; and, whereas the feebler folk are ready to succumb, the bolder spirits face it. Religion is the facing of the unknown. It is the courage in it that brings comfort.

We must go on, however, to consider religion sociologically. A religion is the effort to face crisis, so far as that effort is organized by society in some particular way. A religion is congregational - that is to say, serves the ends of a number of persons simultaneously. It is traditional-that is to say, has served the ends of successive generations of persons.

Therefore inevitably it has standardized a method. It involves a routine, a ritual. Also it involves some sort of conventional doctrine, which is, as it were, the inner side of the ritual-its lining.

Now in what follows in the first instance, on this sociological side of religion. For anthropological purposes it is the sounder plan. We must altogether eschew that "Robinson Crusoe method" which consists in reconstructing the creed of a solitary savage, who is supposed to evolve his religion out of his inner consciousness: "The mountain frowns, therefore it is alive"; "I move about in my dreams whilst my body lies still, therefore I have a soul," and so on. No doubt somebody had to think these things, for they are thoughts. But he did not think them, at any rate did not think them out, alone. Men thought them out together; nay, whole ages of living and thinking together have gone to make them what they are. So a social method is needed to explain them.

The religion of a savage is part of his custom; nay, rather, it is his whole custom so far as it appears sacred-so far as it coerces him by way of his imagination. Between him and the unknown stands nothing but his custom. It is his all-in-all, his stand-by, his faith and his hope. Being thus the sole source of his confidence, his custom, so far as his imagination plays about it, becomes his "luck." We may say that any and every custom, in so far as it is regarded as lucky, is a religious rite.

Hence the conservatism inherent in religion. "Nothing," says Robertson Smith, "appeals so strongly as religion to the conservative instincts." "The history of religion," once exclaimed Dr. Frazer, "is a long attempt to reconcile old custom with new reason, to find a sound theory for absurd practice." At first sight one is apt to see nothing but the absurdities in savage custom and religion. After all, these are what strike us most, being the curiosity-hunters that we all are. But savage custom and religion must be taken as a whole, the bad side with the good. Of course, if we have to do with a primitive society on the down-grade-and very few that have been "civilizaded," as John Stuart Mill terms it, at the hands of the white man are not on the down-grade-its disorganized and debased custom no longer serves a vital function. But a healthy society is bound, in a wholesale way, to have a healthy custom. Though it may go about the business in a queer and roundabout fashion, it must hit off the general requirements of the situation. Therefore I shall not waste time, as I might easily do, in piling up instances of outlandish "superstitions," whether horrible and disgusting, from our more advanced point of view, or merely droll and silly. On the contrary, I would rather make it my working assumption that, with all its apparent drawbacks, the religion of a human society, if the latter be a going concern, is always something to be respected.

In considering, however, the relation of religion to custom, we are met by the apparent difficulty that, whereas custom implies "Do," the prevailing note of primitive religion would seem rather to consist in "Do not." But there is really no antagonism between them on this account. As the old Greek proverb has it, "There is only one way of going right, but there are infinite ways of going wrong." Hence, a nice observance of custom of itself involves endless taboos. Since a given line of conduct is lucky, then this or that alternative course of behaviour must be unlucky. There is just this difference between positive customs or rites, which cause something to be done, and negative customs or rites, which cause something to be left undone, that the latter appeal more exclusively to the imagination for their sanction, and are therefore more conspicuously and directly a part of religion. "Why should I do this?" is answered well-nigh sufficiently by saying, "Because it is the custom, because it is right." It seems hardly necessary to add, "Because it will bring luck." But "Why should I not do something else instead?" meets, in the primitive society, with the invariable answer, "Because, if you do, something awful will happen to us all." What precise shape the ill-luck will take need not be specified. The suggestion rather gains than loses by the indefiniteness of its appeal to the imagination.

To understand more clearly the difference between negative and positive types of custom as associated with religion, let us examine in some detail an example of each. It will be well to select our cases from amongst those that show the custom and the religion to be quite inseparable-to be, in short, but two aspects of one and the same fact. Now nothing could be more commonplace and secular a custom than that of providing for one's dinner. Yet for primitive society this custom tends to be likewise a rite-a rite which may, however, be mainly negative and precautionary, or mainly positive and practical in character, as we shall now see.

The Todas, so well described by Dr. Rivers, are a small community, less than a thousand all told, who have retired out of the stress of the world into the fastnesses of the Nilgiri Hills, in southern India, where they spend a safe but decidedly listless life. They are in a backwater, and are likely to remain there. At any rate, their religion is not such as to make them more enterprising. Gods they may be said to have none. The bare names of certain deities of the hill-tops are retained, but whether these were once the honoured gods of the Todas or, as some think, those of a former race, certain it is that there is more shadow than substance about them now. The real religion of the people centres round a dairy-ritual. From a practical and economic point of view, the work of the dairy consists in converting the milk of their buffaloes into the butter and buttermilk which constitute their staple diet. From a religious point of view, it consists in converting something they dare not eat into something they can eat.

Many, though not all, of their buffaloes are sacred, and their milk may not be drunk. The reason why it may not be drunk anthropologists may cast about to discover, but the Todas themselves do not know. All that they know, and are concerned to know, is that things would somehow all go wrong, if any one were foolish enough to commit such a sin. So in the Toda temple, which is a dairy, the Toda priest, who is the dairyman, sets about rendering the sacred products harmless. The dairy has two compartments-one sacred, the other profane. In the first are stored the sacred vessels, into which the milk is placed when it comes from the buffaloes, and in which it is turned into butter and buttermilk with the help of some of the previous brew, this having meanwhile been put by in an especially sacred vessel. In the second compartment are profane vessels, destined to receive the butter and buttermilk, after they have been carefully transferred from the sacred vessels with the help of an intermediary vessel, which stands exactly on the line between the two compartments. This transference, being carried out to the accompaniment of all sorts of reverential gestures and utterances, secures such a profanation of the sacred substance as is without the evil consequences that would otherwise be entailed. Thus the ritual is essentially precautionary. A taboo is the hinge of the whole affair.

And the tendency of such a negative type of religion is to pile precautions on precautions. Thus the dairyman, in order to be equal to his sacred office, must observe taboos without end. He must be celibate. He must avoid all contact with the dead. He is limited to certain kinds of food; which, moreover, must be prepared in a certain way, and consumed in a certain place. His drink, again, is a special milk, which must be poured out with prescribed formulas. He is inaccessible to ordinary folk save on certain days and in certain ways, their mode of approach, their salutations, his greeting in reply, being all regulated with the utmost nicety. He can only wear a special garb. He must never cut his hair. His nails must be suffered to grow long. And so on and so forth. Such disabilities, indeed, are wont to circumscribe the life of all sacred persons, and can be matched from every part of the world. But they may fairly be cited here, as helping to fill in the picture of what I have called the precautionary or negative type of religious ritual.

Further, there is something rotten in the state of Toda religion. The dairymen struck Dr. Rivers as very slovenly in the performance of their duties, as well as vague and inaccurate in their accounts of what ought to be done. Indeed, it was hard to find persons willing to undertake the office. Ritual duties involving uncomfortable taboos were apt to be thrust on youngsters. The youngsters, being youngsters, would probably violate the taboos; but anyway that was their look-out. From evasions to fictions is but a step. Hence when an unclean person approached the dairyman, the latter would simply pretend not to see him. Or the rule that he must not enter a hut, if women were within, would be circumvented by simply removing from the dwelling the three emblems of womanhood, the pounder, the sieve, and the sweeper; whereupon his "face was saved." Now wherefore all this lack of earnestness? Dr. Rivers thinks that too much ritual was the reason. I agree; but would venture to add, "too much negative ritual." A religion that is all dodging must produce a sneaking kind of worshipper.

Now let us turn another type of primitive religion that is equally identified with the food-quest, but allied to its positive and active functions, which it seeks to help out. Messrs. Spencer and Gillen have given us a most minute account of certain ceremonies of the Arunta, a people of central Australia. These ceremonies they have named 'Intichiuma', and the name will probably stick, though there is reason to believe that the native word for them is really something different. Their purpose is to make the food-animals and food-plants multiply and prosper. Each animal or plant is attended to by the group that has it for a totem. (Totemism amongst this very remarkable people has nothing to do either with exogamy or with lineage; but that is a subject into which it is impossible to go here.) The rites vary considerably from totem to totem, but a typical case or two may be cited.

The witchetty-grub men, for instance, want the grubs to multiply, that there may be plenty for their fellows to eat. So they wend their way along a certain path which tradition declares to have been traversed by the great leader of the witchetty-grubs of the days of long ago. (These were grubs transformed into men, who became by reincarnation ancestors of the present totemites.) The path brings them to a place in the hills where there is a big stone surrounded by many small stones. The big stone is the adult animal, the little stones are its eggs. So first they tap the big stone, chanting an invitation to it to lay eggs. Then the master of the ceremonies rubs the stomach of each totemite with the little stones, and says, "You have eaten much food."

Or, again, the Kangaroo men repair to a place called Undiara. It is a picturesque spot. By the side of a water-hole that is sheltered by a tall gum-tree rises a curiously gnarled and weather-beaten face of quartzite rock. About twenty feet from the base a ledge juts out. When the totemites hold their ceremony, they repair to this ledge. For here in the days of long ago the ancestors who are now reincarnated in them cooked and ate kangaroo food; and here, moreover, the kangaroo animals of that time deposited their spirit-parts. First the face of the rock below the ledge is decorated with long stripes of red ochre and white gypsum, to represent the red fur and white bones of the kangaroo. It is, in fact, one of those rock-paintings such as the palaeolithic men of Europe made in their caves. Then a number of men, say, seven or eight, mount upon the ledge, and, whilst the rest sing solemn chants about the prospective increase of the kangaroos, these men open veins in their arms, so that the blood flows down freely upon the ceremonial stone. This is the first part of the rite. The second part is no less interesting. After the blood-letting, they hunt until they kill a kangaroo. Thereupon the old men of the totem eat a little of the meat; then they smear some of the fat on the bodies of all the party; finally, hey divide the flesh amongst them. Afterwards, the totemites paint their bodies with stripes in imitation of the design upon the rock. A second hunt, followed by a second sacramental meal, concludes the whole ceremony. That their meal is sacramental, a sort of communion service, is proved by the fact that henceforth in an ordinary way they allow themselves to partake of kangaroo meat at most but very sparingly, and of certain portions of the flesh not at all.

One more example of these rites may be cited, in order to bring out the earnestness of this type of religion, which is concerned with doing, instead of mere not-doing. There is none of the Toda perfunctoriness here. It will be enough to glance at the commencement of the ritual of the honey-ant totemites. The master of the ceremonies places his hand as if he were shading his eyes, and gazes intently in the direction of the sacred place to which they are about to repair. As he does so, the rest kneel, forming a straight line behind him. In this position they remain for some time, whilst the leader chants in a subdued tone. Then all stand up. The company must now start. The leader, who has fallen to the rear, that he may marshal the column in perfect line, gives the signal. Then they move off in single file, taking a direct course to the holy ground, marching in perfect silence, and with measured step, as if something of the profoundest import were about to take place.

It is necessary to convey the impression that the essentials of religion are present in these apparently godless observances of the ruder peoples. They arise directly out of custom - in this case the hunting custom. Their immediate design is to provide these people with their daily bread. Yet their appeal to the imagination-which in religion, as in science, art, and philosophy, is the impulse that presides over all progress, all creative evolution-is such that the food-quest is charged with new and deeper meaning. Not bread alone, but something even more sustaining to the life of man, is suggested by these tangled and obscure solemnities. They are penetrated by quickenings of sacrifice, prayer, and communion. They bring to bear on the need of the hour all the promise of that miraculous past, which not only cradled the race, but still yields it the stock of reincarnated soul-force that enables it to survive. If, then, these rites are part and parcel of mere magic, most, or all, of what the world knows as religion must be mere magic. But it is better for anthropology to call things by the names that they are known by in the world of men-that is, in the wider world, not in some corner or coterie of it.

In order to bring out more fully the second point, namely, the close interdependence between religion and custom in primitive society, let me be allowed to quote one more example of the ritual of a rude people. And again let us resort to native Australia, though this time to the south-eastern corner of it;

since in Australia we have a cultural development on the whole very low, having been as it were arrested through isolation, yet one that turns out to be not incompatible with high religion in the making.

Initiation in native Australia is the equivalent of what is known amongst ourselves as the higher education. The only difference is that, with them, every one who is not judged utterly unfit is duly initiated; whereas, with us, the higher education is offered to some who are unfit, whilst many who are fit never have the luck to get it. The initiation-custom is intended to tide the boys over the difficult time of puberty, and turn them into responsible men. The whole of the adult males assist in the ceremonies. Special men, however, are told off to tutor the youth-a lengthy business, since it entails a retirement, perhaps for six months, into the bush with their charges; who are there taught the tribal traditions, and are generally admonished, sometimes forcibly, for their good. Further, this is rather like a retirement into a monastery for the young men, seeing that during all the time they are strictly taboo, or in other words in a holy state that involves much fasting and mortification of the flesh. At last comes the time when their actual passage across the threshold of manhood has to be celebrated. The rites may be described in one word as impressive. Society wishes to set a stamp on their characters, and believes in stamping hard. Physically, then, the lads feel the force of society. A tooth is knocked out, they are tossed in the air to make them grow tall, and so on-rites that, whilst they may have separate occult ends in view, are completely at one in being highly unpleasant.

Spiritual means of education, however, are always more effective than physical, if designed and applied with sufficient wisdom. The bull-roarer, of which something has been already said, furnishes the ceremonies with a background of awe. It fills the woods, that surround the secret spot where the rites are held, with the rise and fall of its weird music, suggestive of a mighty rushing wind, of spirits in the air. Not until the boys graduate as men do they learn how the sound is produced. Even when they do learn this, the mystery of the voice speaking through the chip of wood merely wings the imagination for loftier flights. Whatever else the high god of these mysteries, Daramulun, may be for these people-and undoubtedly all sorts of trains of confused thinking meet in the notion of him-he is at any rate the god of the bull-roarer, who has put his voice into the sacred instrument. But Daramulun is likewise endowed with a human form; for they set up an image of him rudely shaped in wood, and round about it dance and shout his name. Daramulun instituted these rites, as well as all the other immemorial rites of the assembled tribe or tribes. So when over the heads of the boys, prostrated on the ground, are recited solemnly what Mr. Lang calls "the ten commandments," that bid them honour the elders, respect the marriage law, and so on, there looms up before their minds the figure of the ultimate law-giver; whilst his unearthly voice becomes for them the voice of the law. Thus is custom exalted, and its coercive force amplified, by the suggestion of a power - in this case a definitely personal power-that "makes for righteousness," and, whilst beneficent, is full of terror for offenders.

And now it may seem high time to pass on from the sociological and external view that has hitherto been taken of primitive religion to a psychological view of it-one that should endeavour to disclose the hidden motives, the spiritual sources, of the beliefs that underlie and sustain the customary practices. But precisely at this point the anthropological treatment of religion is apt to prove unsatisfactory. History can record that such and such is done with far more certainty than that such and such a state of mind accompanies and inspires the doing. Besides, the savage is no authority on the why and wherefore of his customs. "However else would a reasonable being think of acting?" is his sufficient reason, as we have already seen. Not but what the higher minds amongst savages reflect in their own way upon the meaning of their customs and rites. But most of this reflection is no more than an elaborate "justification after the event." The mind invents what Mr. Kipling would call a "Just-so story" to account for something already there. How it might have come about, not how it did come about, is all that the professed explanation amounts to. And when it comes to choosing amongst mere possibilities, the anthropologist, instead of consulting the savage, may just as well endeavour to do it for himself. Now anthropological theories of the origin of religion seem to me to go wrong mainly because they seek to simplify too much. Having got down to what they take to be a root-idea, they straightway proclaim it 'the root-idea.

ANIMISM

The theory of the origin of religion that may be said to hold the field, because it is the view of the greatest of living anthropologists, is Dr. Tylor's theory of animism. The term animism is derived from the Latin 'anima', which-like the corresponding word 'spiritus', whence our "spirit"-signifies the breath, and hence the soul, which primitive folk tend to identify with the breath. Dr. Tylor's theory of animism, then, as set forth in his great work, 'Primitive Culture', is that "the belief in spiritual beings" will do as a definition of religion taken at its least; which for him means the same thing as taken at its earliest. Now what is a "spiritual being"? Clearly everything turns on that. Dr. Tylor's general treatment of the subject seems to lay most of the emphasis on the phantasm. A phantasm (as the etymology of the word shows) is essentially an appearance. In a dream or hallucination one sees figures, more or less dim, but still having "vaporous materiality." So, too, the shadow is something without body that one can see; though the breath, except on a frosty day, shows its subtle but yet sensible nature rather by being felt than by being seen. Now there can be no doubt that the phantasm plays a considerable part in primitive religion (as well as in those fancies of the primitive mind that have never found their way into religion, at all events into religion as identified with organized cult). Savages see ghosts, though probably not more frequently than we do; they have vivid dreams, and are much impressed by their dream-experiences; and so on. Besides, the phantasm forms a very convenient half-way house between the seen and the unseen; and there can be no doubt that the savage often says breath, shadow, and so forth, when he is trying to think and mean something immaterial altogether.

But animism would seem sometimes to be used by Dr. Tylor in a wider sense, namely, as "a doctrine of universal vitality." In dealing with the myths of the ruder peoples, as, for example, those about the sun, moon, and stars, he shows how "a general animation of nature" is implied. The primitive man reads himself into these things, which, according to our science, are without life or personality. He thinks that they have a different kind of body, but the same kind of feelings and motives. But this is not necessarily to think that they are capable of giving off a phantasm, as a man does when his soul temporarily leaves him, or when after death his soul becomes a ghost. There need be nothing ghost-like about the sun, whether it is imagined as a shining orb, or as a shining being of human shape to whom the orb belongs. There is not anything in the least phantasmal about the Greek god Apollo. I think, then, that we had better distinguish this wider sense of animism by a different name, calling it "animatism," since that will serve at once to disconnect and to connect the two conceptions.

When, on the other hand, the thing, or the person, falls within the world of supernormal experience, when they strike the imagination as wonderful and wonder-working, then there is much more reason why he should seek to account to himself for the mystery in, or behind, the strange appearance. Howitt, who knew his Australian natives intimately, cites the following as "a good example of how the native mind works." To the black-fellow his club or his spear are part and parcel of his ordinary life. There is no, "medicine," no "devil," in them. If they are to be made supernaturally potent, they must be specially charmed. But it is quite otherwise with his spear-thrower or his bull-roarer. The former for no obvious reason enables him to throw his spear extraordinarily far. The latter emits the noise of thunder, though a mere chip of wood on the end of a string. These, then, are in themselves "medicine." There is "virtue" in, or behind, them.

Is, then, to attribute "virtue" the same thing, necessarily, as to attribute vitality? Are the spear-thrower and the bull-roarer inevitably thought of as alive? Or are they, as a matter of course, endowed with soul or spirit? Or may there be also an impersonal kind of "virtue," "medicine," or whatever the wonder-working power in the wonder-working thing is to be called? Now there is evidence that the savage himself, in speaking about these matters, sometimes says power, sometimes vitality, sometimes spirit. But the simplest way of disposing of these questions is to remember that such fine distinctions as these, which theorists may seek to draw, do not appeal at all to the savage himself. For him the only fact that matters is that, whereas some things in the world are ordinary, and can be reckoned on, other things cannot be reckoned on, but are wonder-working.

Moreover, of wonder-working things, some are good and some are bad. To get all the good kind of wonder-workers on to his side, so as to confound the bad kind-that is what his religion is there to do for him. "May blessings come, may mischiefs go!" is the import of his religious striving, whether anthropologists class it as spell or as prayer.

FUNCTION OF RELIGION

Now the function of religion, it has been assumed, is to restore confidence, when man is mazed, and out of his depth, fearful of the mysteries that obtrude on his life, yet compelled, if not exactly wishful, to face them and wrest from them whatever help is in them. This function religion fulfils by what may be described in one word as "suggestion." How the suggestion works psychologically-how, for instance, association of ideas, the so-called "sympathetic magic," predominates at the lower levels of religious experience-is a difficult and technical question which cannot be discussed here. Religion stands by when there is something to be done, and suggests that it can be done well and successfully; nay, that it is being so done. And, when the religion is of the effective sort, the believers respond to the suggestion, and put the thing through. As the Latin poet says, "they can because they think they can."

What, from the anthropological point of view, is the effective sort of religion, the sort that survives because, on the whole, those whom it helps survive? It is dangerous to make sweeping generalizations, but there is at any rate a good deal to be said for classing the world's religions either as mechanical and ineffective, or as spiritual and effective. The mechanical kind offers its consolations in the shape of a set of implements. The "virtue" resides in certain rites and formularies. These, as we have seen, are especially liable to harden into mere mechanism when they are of the negative and precautionary type. The spiritual kind of religion, on the other hand, which is especially associated with the positive and active functions of life, tends to read will and personality into the wonder-working powers that it summons to man's aid. The will and personality in the worshippers are in need not so much of implements as of more will and personality. They get this from a spiritual kind of religion; which in one way or another always suggests a society, a communion, as at once the means and the end of vital betterment.

To say that religion works by suggestion is only to say that it works through the imagination. There is good make-believe as well as bad; and one must necessarily imagine and make-believe in order to will. The more or less inarticulate and intuitional forces of the mind, however, need to be supplemented by the power of articulate reasoning, if the will is to make good its twofold character of a faculty of ends that is likewise a faculty of the means to those ends. Suggestion, in short, must be purged by criticism before it can serve as the guide of the higher life. To bring this point out will be the object of the following chapter.

MORALITY

Space is running out fast, and it is quite impossible to grapple with the details of so vast a subject as primitive morality. For these the reader must consult Dr. Westermarck's monumental treatise, 'The Origin and Development of the Moral Ideas', which brings together an immense quantity of facts, under a clear and comprehensive scheme of headings.

He will discover, by the way, that, whereas customs differ immensely, the emotions, one may even say the sentiments, that form the raw material of morality are much the same everywhere.

Here it will be of most use to sketch the psychological groundwork of primitive morality, as contrasted with morality of the more advanced type. In pursuance of the plan hitherto followed, let us try to move yet another step on from the purely exterior view of human life towards our goal; which is to appreciate the true inwardness of human life - so far at least as this is matter for anthropology, which reaches no farther than the historic method can take it.

It is, of course, open to question whether either primitive or advanced morality is sufficiently of one piece to allow, as it were, a composite photograph to be framed of either. For our present purposes, however, this expedient is so serviceable as to be worth risking. Let us assume, then, that there are two main stages in the historical evolution of society, as considered from the standpoint of the psychology of conduct and to term them the synnomic and the syntelic phases of society. "Synnomic" (from the Greek 'nomos', custom) means that customs are shared. "Syntelic" (from the Greek 'telos', end) means that ends are shared.

The synnomic phase is, from the psychological point of view, a kingdom of habit; the syntelic phase is a kingdom of reflection. The former is governed by a subconscious selection of its standards of good and bad; the latter by a conscious selection of its standards. It remains to show very briefly how such a difference comes about.

The outstanding fact about the synnomic life of the ruder peoples is perhaps this-that there is hardly any privacy. Of course, many other drawbacks must be taken into account also-no wide-thrown communications, no analytic language, no writing, no books, and so on; but perhaps being in a crowd all the time is the worst drawback of all. For, as Disraeli says in 'Sybil', gregariousness is not association. Constant herding and huddling together hinders the development of personality. That independence of character which is the prime condition of syntelic society cannot mature, even though the germs be there. No one has a chance of withdrawing into his own soul. Therefore the individual does not experience that silent conversation with self which is reflection. Instead of turning inwards, he turns outwards. In short, he imitates.

But how, it may be objected, does evolution take place, if every one imitates every one else? Certainly, it looks at first sight like a vicious circle. Nevertheless, there is room for a certain progress, or at any rate for a certain process of change. To analyse its psychological springs would take us too long. If a phrase will do instead of an explanation, we may sum them up, with the brilliant French psychologist, Tarde, as "a cross-fertilization of imitations." We need not, however, go far to get an impression of how this process of change works. It is going on every day in our midst under the name of "change of fashion." When one purchases the latest thing in ties or straw hats, one is not aiming at a rational form of dress. If there is progress in this direction, it is subconscious. The underlying spiritual condition is not inaptly described by Dr. Lloyd Morgan as "a sheep-through-the-gapishness."

From a moral point of view, this lack of capacity for private judgment is equivalent to a want of moral freedom. We have seen how relatively external are the sanctions of savage life. This does not mean, of course, that there is no answering judgment in the mind of the individual when he follows his customs. He says, "It is the custom; therefore it is right." But this judgment can scarcely be said to proceed from a truly judging, that is to say, critical, self. The man watches his neighbours, taking his cue from them. His judgment is a judgment of sense. He does not look inwards to principle. A moral principle is a standard that can, by means of thought, be transferred from one sensible situation to another sensible situation. The general law, and its application to the situation present now to the senses, are considered apart, before being put together. Consequently, a possible application, however strongly suggested by custom, fashion, the action of one's neighbours, one's own impulse or prejudice, or what not, can be resisted, if it appear on reflection not to be really suited to the circumstances. In short, in order to be rational and "put two and two together," one must be able to entertain two and two as distinct conceptions. Perceptions, on the contrary, can only be compared in the lump. Just as in the chapter on language we saw how man began by talking in holophrases, and only gradually attained to analytic, that is, separable, elements of speech, so in this chapter we have to note the strictly parallel development from confusion to distinction on the side of thought.

Savage morality, then, is not rational in the sense of analysed, but is, so to speak, impressionistic. We might, perhaps, describe it as the expression of a collective impression. It is best understood in the light of that branch of social psychology which usually goes by the name of "mob-psychology." Perhaps mob and mobbish are rather unfortunate terms. They are apt to make us think of the wilder explosions of collective feeling-panics, blood-mania, dancing-epidemics, and so on. But, though a savage society is by no means a mob in the sense of a weltering mass of humanity that has for the time being lost its head, the psychological considerations applying to the latter apply also to the former, when due allowance has been made for the fact that savage society is organized on a permanent basis. The difference between the two comes, in short, to this, that the mob as represented in the savage society is a mob consisting of many successive generations of men. Its tradition constitutes, as it were, a prolonged and abiding impression, which its conduct thereupon expresses.

Savage thought, then, is not able, because it does not try, to break up custom into separate pieces. Rather it plays round the edges of custom; religion especially, with its suggestion of the general sacredness of custom, helping it to do so. There is found in primitive society plenty of vague speculation that seeks to justify the existing. But to take the machine to bits in order to put it together differently is out of the reach of a type of intelligence which, though competent to grapple with details, takes its principles for granted. When progress comes, it comes by stealth, through imitating the letter, but refusing to imitate the spirit; until by means of legal fictions, ritual substitutions, and so on, the new takes the place of the old without any one noticing the fact.

Freedom, in the sense of intellectual freedom, may perhaps be said to have been born in one place and at one time-namely, in Greece in the fifth and fourth centuries B.C. Of course, minglings and clashings of peoples had prepared the way. Ideas begin to count as soon as they break away from their local context. But Greece, in teaching the world the meaning of intellectual freedom, paved a way towards that most comprehensive form of freedom which is termed moral. Moral freedom is the will to give out more than you take in; to repay with interest the cost of your social education. It is the will to take thought about the meaning and end of human life, and by so doing to assist in creative evolution.

MAN AS INDIVIDUAL

By way of epilogue, a word about individuality, as displayed amongst peoples of the ruder type, will not be out of place. There is a real danger lest the anthropologist should think that a scientific view of man is to be obtained by leaving out the human nature in him. This comes from the over-anxiety of evolutionary history to arrive at general principles. It is too ready to rule out the so-called "accident," forgetful of the fact that the whole theory of biological evolution may with some justice be described as "the happy accident theory." The man of high individuality, then, the exceptional man, the man of genius, be he man of thought, man of feeling, or man of action, is no accident that can be overlooked by history. On the contrary, he is in no small part the history-maker; and, as such, should be treated with due respect by the history-compiler. The "dry bones" of history, its statistical averages, and so on, are all very well in their way; but they correspond to the superficial truth that history repeats itself, rather than to the deeper truth that history is an evolution. Anthropology, then, should not disdain what might be termed the method of the historical novel. To study the plot without studying the characters will never make sense of the drama of human life.

It may seem a truism, but is perhaps worth recollecting at the start, that no man or woman lacks individuality altogether, even if it cannot be regarded in a particular case as a high individuality. No one is a mere item. That useful figment of the statistician has no real existence under the sun. We need to supplement the books of abstract theory with much sympathetic insight directed towards men and women in their concrete selfhood. Said a Vedda cave-dweller to Dr. Seligmann: "It is pleasant for us to feel the rain beating on our shoulders, and good to go out and dig yams, and come home wet, and see the fire burning in the cave, and sit round it." That sort of remark, to my mind, throws more light on the anthropology of cave-life than all the bones and stones that helped to dig out of our Mousterian caves in Jersey. As the stock phrase has it, it is, as far as it goes, a "human document." The individuality, in the sense of the intimate self-existence, of the speaker and his group-for, characteristically enough, he uses the first person plural-is disclosed sufficiently for our souls to get into touch. We are the nearer to appreciating human history from the inside.

Some of those students of mankind, therefore, who have been privileged to live amongst the ruder peoples, and to learn their language well, and really to be friends with some of them (which is hard, since friendship implies a certain sense of equality on both sides), should try their hands at anthropological biography. Anthropology, so far as it relates to savages, can never rise to the height of the most illuminating kind of history until this is done.

It ought not to be impossible for an intelligent white man to enter sympathetically into the mental outlook of the native man of affairs, the more or less practical and hardheaded legislator and statesman, if only complete confidence could be established between the two. That there are men of outstanding individuality who help to make political history even amongst the rudest peoples is, moreover, hardly to be doubted. Thus Messrs. Spencer and Gillen, in the introductory chapter of their work on the Central Australians, state that, after observing the conduct of a great gathering of the natives, they reached the opinion that the changes which undoubtedly take place from time to time in aboriginal custom are by no means wholly of the subconscious and spontaneous sort, but are in part due also to the influence of individuals of superior ability. "At this gathering, for example, some of the oldest men were of no account; but, on the other hand, others not so old as they were, but more learned in ancient lore or more skilled in matters of magic, were looked up to by the others, and they it was who settled everything. It must, however, be understood that we have no definite proof to bring forward of the actual introduction by this means of any fundamental change of custom. The only thing that we can say is that, after carefully watching the natives during the performance of their ceremonies and endeavouring as best we could to enter into their feelings, to think as they did, and to become for the time being one of themselves, we came to the conclusion that if one or two of the most powerful men settled upon the advisability of introducing some change, even an important one, it would be quite possible for this to be agreed upon and carried out."

This passage is worth quoting at length if only for the admirable method that it discloses. The policy of "trying to become for the time being one of themselves" resulted in the book that, of all first-hand studies, has done most for modern anthropology. At the same time Messrs. Spencer and Gillen, it is evident, would not claim to have done more than interpret the external signs of a high individuality on the part of these prominent natives. It still remains a rare and almost unheard-of thing for an anthropologist to be on such friendly terms with a savage as to get him to talk intimately about himself, and reveal the real man within.

There exist, however, occasional side-lights on human personality in the anthropological literature that has to do with very rude peoples. The page from a human document that cite by way of example is all the more curious, because it relates to a type of experience quite outside the compass of ordinary civilized folk. Here and there, however, something like it may be found amongst ourselves. My friend Mr. L.P. Jacks, for instance, in his story-book, 'Mad Shepherds', has described a rustic of the north of England who belonged to this old-world order of great men. For men of the type in question can be great, at any rate in low-level society. The so-called medicine man is a leader, perhaps even the typical leader, of primitive society; and, just because he is, by reason of his calling, addicted to privacy and aloofness, he certainly tends to be more individual, more of a "character," than the general run of his fellows.

The Wiradjuri doctor of the Kangaroo totem said: "My father is a Lizard-man. When I was a small boy, he took me into the bush to train me to be a doctor. He placed two large quartz-crystals against my breast, and they vanished into me. I do not know how they went, but I felt them going through me like warmth. This was to make me clever, and able to bring things up." (This refers to the medicine-man's custom of bringing up into the mouth, as if from the stomach, the quartz-crystal in which his "virtue" has its chief material embodiment or symbol; being likewise useful, as we see later on, for hypnotizing purposes.) "He also gave me some things like quartz-crystals in water. They looked like ice, and the water tasted sweet. After that, I used to see things that my mother could not see. When out with her I would say, 'What is out there like men walking?' She used to say, 'Child, there is nothing.' These were the ghosts which I began to see."

The account goes on to state that at puberty our friend went through the regular initiation for boys; when he saw the doctors bringing up their crystals, and, crystals in mouth, shooting the "virtue" into him to make him "good." Thereupon, being in a holy state like any other novice, he had retired to the bush in the customary manner to fast and meditate.

"Whilst I was in the bush, my old father came out to me. He said, 'Come here to me,' and then he showed me a piece of quartz-crystal in his hand. When I looked at it, he went down into the ground; and I saw him come up all covered with red dust. It made me very frightened. Then my father said, 'Try and bring up a crystal.' I did try, and brought one up. He then said, 'Come with me to this place.' I saw him standing by a hole in the ground, leading to a grave. I went inside and saw a dead man, who rubbed me all over to make me clever, and gave me some crystals. When we came out, my father pointed to a tiger-snake, saying, 'That is your familiar. It is mine also.' There was a string extending from the tail of the snake to us-one of those strings which the medicine-men bring up out of themselves. My father took hold of the string, and said, 'Let us follow the snake.' The snake went through several tree-trunks, and let us through them. At last we reached a tree with a great swelling round its roots. It is in such places that Daramulun lives. The snake went down into the ground, and came up inside the tree, which was hollow. We followed him. There I saw a lot of little Daramuluns, the sons of Baiame. Afterwards, the snake took us into a great hole, in which were a number of snakes. These rubbed themselves against me, and did not hurt me, being my familiars. They did this to make me a clever man and a doctor.

"Then my father said, 'We will go up to Baiame's Camp.' [Amongst the Wiradjuri, Baiame is the high god, and Daramulun is his son. What 'little Daramuluns' may be is not very clear.] He got astride a thread, and put me on another, and we held by each other's arms. At the end of the thread was Wombu, the bird of Baiame. We went up through the clouds, and on the other side was the sky. We went through the place where the doctors go through, and it kept opening and shutting very quickly. My father said that, if it touched a doctor when he was going through, it would hurt his spirit, and when he returned home he would sicken and die. On the other side we saw Baiame sitting in his camp. He was a very great old man with a long beard. He sat with his legs under him, and from his shoulders extended two great quartz-crystals to the sky above him. There were also numbers of the boys of Baiame, and of his people who are birds and beasts.

Bibliography

Andrews, Peggy. *Sisters Listening to Sisters: Women of the World Share Stories of Personal Empowerment.* Bergin and Garvey, 1996.

Awkward, Michael. *Negotiating Difference: Race, Gender, and the Politics of Positionality.* University of Chicago Press, 1995.

Bannerji, Himani, ed. *Returning the Gaze: Essays on Racism, Feminism, and Politics.* Sister Vision Press, 1993.

Bannerji, Himani. *Thinking Through: Essays on Feminism, Marxism, and Anti-Racism.* Women's Press, 1995.

Butler, Judith and Joan W. Scott, ed. *Feminists Theorize the Political.* Routledge, 1992.

Chapman, Jennifer. *Politics, Feminism and the Reformation of Gender.* Routledge, 1992.

Chapman, Jenny. *Politics, Feminism and the Reformation of Gender.* Routledge, 1993.

Daniels, Cynthia R., ed. *Feminists Negotiate the State: The Politics of Domestic Violence.* University Press of America, 1997.

Elman, R. Amy, ed. *Sexual Politics and the European Union: The New Feminist Challenge.* Berghahn Books, 1996.

Elshtain, Jean Bethke. *Meditations on Modern Political Thought: Masculine/Feminine Themes from Luther to Arendt.* Penn State Univ. Press, 1992.

Fowlkes, Diane L. *White Political Women: Paths from Privilege to Empowerment.* Univ. of Tennessee Press, 1992.

Fraser, Nancy. *Justice Interruptus: Critical Reflections on the "Postsocialist" Condition.* Routledge, 1997.

Gottfried, Heidi, ed. *Feminism and Social Change: Bridging Theory and Practice.* Univ. of Illinois Press, 1996.

Gunew, Sneja and Anna Yeatman, ed. *Feminism and the Politics of Difference.* (out of print)

Hawkesworth, M.E. *Beyond Oppression: Feminist Theory and Political Strategy.* (out of print)

Hirschmann, Nancy J. and Christine DiStefano, ed. *Revisioning the Political: Feminist Reconstructions of Traditional Concepts in Western Political Theory.* Westview Press.

Hughes-Freeland, Felicia and Nickie Charles, ed. *Practising Feminism: Identity, Difference and Power.* Routledge, 1996.

Jaggar, Alison, ed. *Feminist Politics and Human Nature.* Rowman and Littlefield, 1983.

Jagger, Alison M. *Feminist Politics and Human Nature.* Rowman and Littlefield, 1983.

Jenefsky, Cindy and Ann Russo. *Without Apology: Andrea Dworkin's Art and Politics.* Westview Press, 1997.

Jensen, Pamela Grande, ed. *Finding a New Feminism: Rethinking the Woman Question for Liberal Democracy.* Rowman and Littlefield, 1996.

Jensen, Pamela Grande, ed. *Finding a New Feminism: Rethinking the Woman Question for Liberal Democracy.* Rowman and LIttlefield, 1996.

Jones, Kathleen B. and Anna G. Jónasdóttir, ed. *The Political Interests of Gender: Developing Theory and Research with a Feminist Face.* Sage, 1988.

Jones, Kathleen B., ed. *Citizenship in Feminism: Identity, Action, and Locale.* Indiana University Press, 1998.

Kaplan, Temma. *Crazy for Democracy: Women in Grassroots Movements.* Routledge, 1997.

Kenney, Sally J. and Helen Kinsella, ed. *Politics and Feminist Standpoint Theories.* Haworth Press, 1997.

King, Katie. *Theory in Its Feminist Travels: Conversations in U.S. Women's Movements.* Indiana Univ. Press, 1994.

Marshall, Barbara L. *Engendering Modernity: Feminism, Social Theory, and Social Change.* Northeastern Univ. Press, 1994.

Marshall, Catherine, ed. *Feminist Critical Policy Analysis.* Falmer Press, 1997.

Matthews, Donald G. and Jane S. DeHart. *Sex, Gender, and the Politics of ERA: A State and the Nation.* 1990.

McDonald, Lynn, ed. *Women Theorists on Society and Politics.* Wilfrid Laurier University Press, 1998.

Monk, Janice and Maria Dolors, ed. *Women of the European Union.* Routledge, 1996.

Naples, Nancy A. *Grassroots Warriors: Activist Mothering, Community Work, and the War on Poverty.* Routledge, 1998.

Newton, Judith. *Starting Over: Feminism and the Politics of Cultural Critique.* Univ. of Michigan Press, 1994.

Norris, Pippa, ed. *Women, Media, and Politics.* Oxford, 1998.

Okin, Susan Moller. *Women in Western Political Thought.* Princeton Univ. Press, 1992.

Pascall, Gillian. *Social Policy: A New Feminist Analysis.* 1997.

Pateman, Carole. *Participation and Democratic Theory.* Cambridge Univ. Press, 1970.

Pateman, Carole. *The Disorder of Women: Democracy, Feminism and Political Theory.* Stanford Univ. Press, 1989.

Pateman, Carole. *The Problem of Political Obligation: A Critical Analysis of Liberal Theory.* John Wiley and Son, 1979.

Phillips, Anne. *Engendering Democracy.* Penn State Univ. Press, 1991.

Randall, Vicky and Georgina Waylen, ed. *Gender, Politics and the State.* NY: Routledge, 1998.

Staudt, Kathleen. *Managing Development: State, Society, and International Contexts.* Sage, 1991. (Fourth printing, 1996).

Staudt, Kathleen. *Policies, Politics and Gender: Women Gaining Ground.* Kumarian Press, 1998.

Staudt, Kathleen. *Political Science and Feminisms: Integration or Transformation?* (co-authored with William Weaver). Twayne/MacMillan, 1997.

Sunstein, Cass R., ed. *Feminism and Political Theory.* Univ. of Chicago Press, 1990.

Thomas, Sue and Clyde Wilcox, ed. *Women and Elective Office.* Oxford, 1997.

Thomas, Sue. *How Women Legislate.* Oxford, 1994.

Tobias, Sheila. *Faces of Feminism: An Activist's Reflections on the Women's Movement.* 1997.

Waring, Wendy, ed. *By, For and About: Feminist Cultural Politics.* Women's Press, 1994.

Warren, Karen J. and Duane L. Cady, ed. *Bringing Peace Home: Feminism, Violence, and Nature.* Indiana Univ. Press, 1996.

Wolf, Naomi. *Fire with Fire: The New Female Power and How It Will Change the 21st Century.* Fawcett Books, 1993.

Young, Iris Marion. *Intersecting Voices: Dilemmas of Gender, Political Philosophy, and Policy.* Princeton, 1998.

Young, Iris Marion. *Justice and the Politics of Difference.* Princeton, 1998.

Young, Stacey. *Changing the wor(l)d: Discourse, Politics, and the Feminist Movement.* Routledge, 1997.

Zack, Naomi, Crispin Sartwell and Laurie Shrage, ed. *Race, Class, Gender and Sexuality: The Big Questions.* Blackwell Pub., 1998.

Zack, Naomi, ed. *American Mixed Race: The Culture of Microdiversity.* Rowman and Littlefield, 1995

Index

A

B

C

D

E

F

U

V

W